Conditioning For

Marathon Runners
and Endurance Athletes

Conditioning For
Marathon Runners
and Endurance Athletes

Michael A. Winch
Foreword by David Sunderland

First published in 2006 by
The Crowood Press Ltd
Ramsbury, Marlborough
Wiltshire SN8 2HR

www.crowood.com

British Library Cataloguing-in-Publication Data
A catalogue record for this book is available from the British Library.

ISBN-10 1 86126 901 3
ISBN-13 978 1 86126 901 0

Disclaimer
Please note that the author and the publisher of this book do not
accept any responsibility whatsoever for any error or omission, nor
any loss, injury, damage, adverse outcome or liability suffered as a
result of the information contained in this book, or reliance upon it.
Since conditioning exercises can be dangerous and could involve
physical activities that are too strenuous for some individuals to
engage in safely, it is essential that a doctor be consulted before
undertaking training.

Acknowledgements
I would like to acknowledge the superb help in writing this book
from my wife Carole, who has pushed me hard to complete the work
even though at times I have struggled. I would also like to thank a
number of the athletes I coach who have helped with the
photographs and other aspects of the book.

Edited and designed by Outhouse!
Shalbourne, Marlborough, Wiltshire SN8 3QJ

Printed and bound in Spain by GraphyCems

Contents

Foreword

Having known Mike Winch for a great many years I can think of no one better who could write a book on conditioning for marathon runners and endurance athletes. It therefore gives me great pleasure to write the foreword to this book, which is essential reading for all athletes and coaches who are searching for that extra element of training that will help them fulfil their potential. Conditioning is an essential part of training but it is often neglected by endurance athletes and coaches alike. This book will assist them in taking that little extra step to further their ambitions and give them the edge over their competitors.

Conditioning should be an essential part of all endurance athletes' training schedules. In this book Mike has covered every aspect of conditioning that an endurance runner could utilize. Ranging from the expected aerobic and anaerobic training associated with marathon and endurance runners, through to the often overlooked essentials such as core stability, mobility, posture and technique. Added

to this, there are important chapters on how to include and develop circuit training, weight training, testing and measuring in a training schedule.

If for example you are running a marathon for well over two hours in duration, technique and mobility are essential requirements, but these can only be maximized and fully maintained throughout the competition if they are underpinned by a thorough conditioning programme. It is equally as important for all athletes in the other endurance events to include conditioning in their training programmes. This is especially so during a long season, a double periodized year and for major championships where a number of rounds have to be negotiated on consecutive days.

This book will not only highlight the importance of conditioning for endurance runners, but also help fill a vacuum in this area. It is therefore with great pleasure that I recommend this book to both endurance coaches and athletes alike.

David Sunderland
Former National Events
Coach (Endurance)

Introduction

This book has been written very much with the coach and athlete in mind, neither of whom may be experts in conditioning or have any idea of the wide variety of very helpful exercises and schedule types that can aid effective progress. Endurance athletes need as much conditioning to perform their chosen event as any other athlete. The problem they face, however, is that their basic training must involve extensive running if they are to improve their aerobic capacity. This means that little time is available to perform the essential body conditioning that is required to help prevent injury and maximize performance. Unfortunately, this paradoxical situation leads many endurance athletes to ignore those very techniques and methods that would actually help them achieve better results.

Paula Radcliffe has not achieved such magnificent success merely by running every day; in addition, she performs core stability and strength training to a very high level of competency. Combined with her phenomenal application to her basic endurance work, this additional training has made Paula one of the greatest, if not the greatest, female endurance athletes of all time. Paula's results alone should motivate all those involved in endurance events to reappraise their schedules and include the conditioning work that will ensure their future success. While it may come as no surprise that Paula can outperform many men in the gym, some people will be less aware that the tricky mid-region exercises she practises to ensure correct posture and strength during her run-

Marathon runners.
(COURTESY OF WEBSHOTS.COM)

7

ning also mean that she can outperform many male endurance athletes on the track.

Endurance events are by definition repetitive, and repetitive strain injuries are a hazard of performing them at even the lowest level. A marathon requires the athlete to take 14,000–18,000 paces with each leg. This amazing statistic demonstrates that even if there is a slight imbalance in running action or posture, it will be repeated tens of thousands of times in each race, and many more if you also consider the training leading up to the event. Even if the problems are minute, they will be magnified enormously simply through repetition. This indicates that great care must be taken in developing the precision of action, balance and posture that are the hallmark of a successful endurance athlete. Gone are the days when the aerobic capacity gained from simply running, swimming, cycling or rowing allowed an athlete to reach the top level of performance. Conditioning is now an essential part of training, and the techniques and methods developed in recent years to help prevent imbalance and injury are as much part of the yearly programme as is the endurance base.

It is no surprise that many of the world's top endurance athletes come from countries where children travel to school on foot, and must walk or run if they wish to travel any distance. This early aerobic conditioning provides a solid base for later achievement, and the varied surfaces on which the youngsters run provides additional conditioning for balance, stability and technique in the running action. The general observation that the majority of African runners look relaxed and technically very proficient is a clear reflection of the essential nature of running in their upbringing. In western culture, walking is more prevalent in youngsters than running, and even that is being curtailed by the use of motor transportation. There is a clear growing gap between the two cultures, and this is unlikely to diminish without a major effort on the part of parents and schools in raising the basic fitness and physical skill levels of our children. Obviously, this also makes Paula's achievements all the more remarkable, and is a tribute to her training methods and sheer tenacity.

This book aims to stimulate ideas on how to approach the subject of body conditioning through wide-ranging descriptions of techniques, methods and session plans applicable to endurance events. It cannot be fully comprehensive and does not attempt to be, but it does cover all the major areas of interest and lays down the principles by which the coach or athlete can develop his or her own routines.

CHAPTER 1
Basic Aerobic Conditioning

Until recently, the specificity of aerobic training had not been fully appreciated. It was assumed that anything that increased the heart rate would have a universal effect on improving aerobic capacity in all activities. To a limited extent this is true, but there is much less of a crossover than was previously thought. The triathlon attests to this specificity: athletes competing in this most strenuous of sports rarely excel at all three events, even though they are all aerobic.

The reason for this specificity is simple – the movements involve very different muscles and techniques. Running is basically isotonic (the limbs accelerate and decelerate during the required movements), but cycling and swimming have a large isokinetic component (the limbs move at even speeds with little acceleration or deceleration). The muscles therefore, by dint of the different techniques used in the events, operate in quite different ways. In consequence, cycling training will improve only the basic aerobic pathways but not the specific aspects of running or swimming. Similarly, swimming will not help the specifics of running or cycling, and running will not improve the specifics of the other two forms of aerobic activity.

This simple truth is ignored by many endurance athletes, who spend too much time using alternatives to running in an effort to help their performance without realizing that only a minimal positive effect will result. As a

Triathletes. (COURTESY OF WEBSHOTS.COM)

Swimmers. (COURTESY OF WEBSHOTS.COM)

Cyclists. (COURTESY OF WEBSHOTS.COM)

Wheelchair triathlete.
(COURTESY OF WEBSHOTS.COM)

rule of thumb, the closer the training exercise is to the sport, the greater the beneficial effect. Put simply, this means that runners should run, cyclists should cycle and swimmers should swim for the most beneficial effects. This specificity of exercise is well understood by triathletes, and to them represents the major challenge of a sport that is the fastest growing in the world and has a strong following of both able-bodied and alternatively abled athletes.

One scenario where aerobic alternatives can be useful is during rehabilitation. When a running injury occurs, for example, the basic levels of aerobic fitness can be maintained to some extent by performing cycling, swimming and even rowing. without placing further strain on the damaged areas.

THE BASIC PHYSIOLOGY OF AEROBIC ACTIVITY

A knowledge of the physiology of aerobic exercise is essential to the athlete and coach training for endurance events. The body is able to work for extended periods of time on the basis of generating useful energy from carbohydrate, amino acid (from protein) and fat sources of food. Diet is, therefore, a key factor affecting an athlete's ability to run aerobically, and the digestive system and metabolism are the intermediates through which food is converted into useful energy.

To perform this conversion of food to energy in the long term, as when running for extended periods, oxygen is needed to complete the biochemical links along the way. In its simplest form, glucose is broken down by combining with oxygen to yield carbon dioxide, water and a high-energy compound called adenosine triphosphate (ATP). This substance is remarkable for its ability to transfer its energy to stimulate muscle contraction. The basic equation for the overall chemical reaction is as follows:

$C_6H_{12}O_6$ (glucose) + $6O_2$ (oxygen) $\rightarrow$ $6H_2O$ (water) + $6CO_2$ (carbon dioxide) + ATP (high-energy compound)

This process involves three main stages: the breakdown of glucose through glycolysis; the conversion of the resulting breakdown products to primary high-energy compounds via the Kreb's cycle (this is the stage during which oxygen is used by the system); and the formation of ATP through oxidative phosphorylation.

All of these processes are mediated by enzymes, which are proteins that are able to speed up biochemical reactions. Proteins themselves are made up of many amino acids linked together in a specific order, this being determined by the genes that make up DNA (deoxyribonucleic acid). In humans, DNA holds the code for more than a hundred thousand proteins, many of which are enzymes, each mediating a specific biochemical reaction. These enzymes are present in minute concentrations in every cell and their levels vary depending on the demands made on the cells for energy. Movement, for example, is produced by muscle contraction, which requires significant energy.

The adaptive process stimulated by training causes an increase in the levels of enzymes involved in energy production. However, these changes are not permanent and so training exercises must be performed consistently and repetitively for the adaptation to be maintained. This is the essence of the biochemical effects of aerobic training. The physiological effects include the following:

1. Improvements in the efficiency of breathing.
2. Improvements in the efficiency of the heart's pumping action.
3. Improvements in the transfer of oxygen from the air in the lungs to the blood, and from the blood to the muscle tissue via the intercellular fluid.
4. Improvements in the transfer of carbon dioxide from the muscles to the blood via the intercellular fluid, and from the blood to the air in the lungs.

The first two of these improvements are discussed in more detail below.

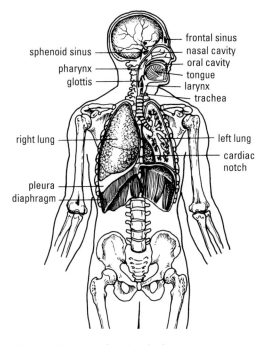

Fig. 1 Diagram showing body section with key respiratory structures labelled.

frontal sinus
sphenoid sinus
nasal cavity
pharynx
oral cavity
glottis
tongue
larynx
trachea
right lung
left lung
cardiac notch
pleura
diaphragm

EFFICIENCY OF BREATHING

The muscles used during breathing are mainly the intercostal muscles between the ribs, and the diaphragm, which is a sheet of muscle separating the thorax from the abdomen and is also attached to the ribcage (*see* Fig. 1). These muscles are controlled by the autonomic (automatic) nervous system from the medulla oblongata (brain stem). The rate and depth of breathing are themselves controlled

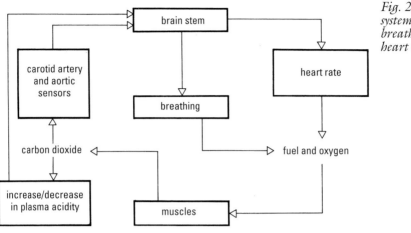

Fig. 2 Biofeedback systems controlling breathing and heart rate.

by biofeedback receptors in the carotid arteries of the neck, which measure the level of carbon dioxide in the blood that passes them.

Biofeedback is a process used by the body to control the way in which it functions. It can be generally defined as a system whereby a measurable stimulus is assessed by receptors in the body, which then respond to the stimulus either by increasing or decreasing an action elsewhere in the body. Our breathing response to exercise is a good example of this system in action (*see* Fig. 2). The automatic response system can be overridden by conscious stimulation of the muscles, but this eliminates the fine control that the biofeedback sensors can apply.

As we have seen, a waste product created through aerobic activity is carbon dioxide. This is removed from the muscle tissue via the blood. In the biofeedback mechanism, an increase in carbon dioxide and a decrease in oxygen dissolved in the plasma of the blood stimulate breathing as the blood passes the carotid and aortic sensors. Likewise, when exercise slows or stops and the carbon dioxide in the blood falls and oxygen increases, the sensors detect this and cause a slow-down in breathing. In addition, any rise in carbon dioxide produces an increase in the blood plasma acidity. This is

detected by sensors on the surface of the brain stem, again stimulating breathing. These simple yet effective systems control breathing during all aerobic exercise.

EFFICIENCY OF THE HEART'S PUMPING ACTION

The heart is a muscle that operates aerobically, pumping blood around the body's circulatory system during normal life. It is suffused with a mass of small blood vessels and capillaries. When aerobic activity increases over a period of time, the number of these capillaries is increased, leading to improved oxygen supply to the heart itself. In turn, this increases the efficiency of the heart and therefore the ease with which it pumps blood in normal life as well as during exercise. It is generally considered that even performing twenty to thirty minutes of low-level steady-paced exercise each day is sufficient to improve the capillarization of the heart and therefore its efficiency of operation.

The normal resting pulse rate (heart rate) should be within the range of forty-five to sixty-five beats per minute, but for the aerobic athlete it may be lower than this or at least at the lower end of the range. Generally speaking, as a person trains aerobically, their resting pulse rate declines. The resting pulse is also a good indicator of general health, since it rises significantly during illness as the body fights to return to normal.

In addition, the resting pulse rate can be used as an indicator of whether the body has recovered sufficiently from the previous day's training. If the recovery is incomplete, the resting pulse will be in excess of the usual resting level by a number of beats. As a general guideline, if this increase is more than five beats per minute then more rest is indicated before normal training should be resumed. This is not a hard and fast rule, but is a useful addition to the other tests and assessments that must be performed by a high-level athlete to monitor progress and recovery status. Unfortunately, there is no reliable science-based indicator of overtraining, so it is down to the skill of the coach to prevent the debilitating slumps in performance that inevitably occur when the body is not allowed sufficient recovery.

As we grow older, the maximum rate at which the heart can beat (HRmax) reduces roughly according to the following formula:

$$\text{HRmax (beats per minute)} = 220 \text{ minus the age in years}$$

Or, more accurately:

$$\text{HRmax} = 205.8 - (0.685 \times \text{age})$$

This latter formula has been found to have a standard of error, which although large (6.4 beats per minute) is still deemed to be acceptable for prescribing HRmax ranges during exercise training. Using the first, simpler formula, the maximum heart rate of a person aged twenty will be around 200, while that of a person aged fifty will be only 170. The formulae help us define the rates at which the heart must beat in order to be at an effective training level.

The graph on page 14, which has been prepared using data collected over a considerable period of time, shows the generally accepted ranges of heart rate during training. These training ranges fall into three main bands:

1. Low aerobic training range (60–75 per cent of HRmax). This defines the heart-rate band within which the athlete must remain to improve aerobic ability, and is achieved through low-level steady exercise.
2. High aerobic training range (75–85 per cent of HRmax). This defines the band within which the athlete must remain to improve aerobic ability further, and is achieved by performing exercise that is at a higher intensity but of shorter duration.
3. Anaerobic training range (≥85 per cent of HRmax). This defines the band of heart rates at which, during training, the aerobic system cannot cope and anaerobic processes kick in to help supply the necessary energy for exercise to continue. During this level of work, lactic acid is formed and rapidly reaches sufficient concentrations in the blood and cells to cause exercise to slow and finally stop.

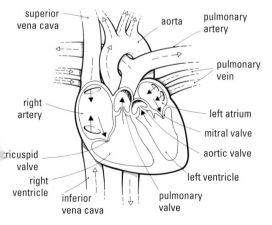

Fig. 3 The heart.

These basic definitions allow an athlete of any age to assess his or her level of training and the results it will have. The method is, of course, simplistic but nevertheless it is very valuable as a raw indicator of effort and results.

SCIENCE AND AEROBIC SPORT

Aerobic exercise, although seemingly simple, is in fact complex, and even the best and most well prepared athlete can have mysterious losses of form and decreases in performance. The coach can prepare only for what is known from the science, most of which has been well researched. However, this has not stopped the continuous search for novel methods of training and improving performance. Human nature being what it is, the search for perfection will continue. This is what makes sports science the growing subject of interest in many countries, and leads cheats to seek methods to circumvent the rules and steal a march on their rivals, for glory or gain.

The misuse of science is an ever-present problem, not only in endurance events but in all sports. The use of performance-enhancing drugs and protocols has been with us since the dawn of sporting endeavour – the ancient Greeks used training, special diets and herbal enhancement to improve results, while today we have erythropoetin (EPO), steroids and blood doping. The playing field has never been level, but at least the new millennium has seen renewed effort to root out sport's wrong-doers.

SUMMARY

- Aerobic training is complex and varied. The returns from even the hardest workouts will be minimal if the specificity of such training is not fully appreciated and applied to the programme. This is clearly exemplified by the sport of triathlon.
- The key to successful aerobic training is its consistent and repetitive performance. Even at the lowest level of such training, the body benefits from improved breathing and cardiovascular efficiency.
- The use of heart-rate monitoring is a simple way of judging the level of exercise needed for improvement and the specific effect of that exercise.

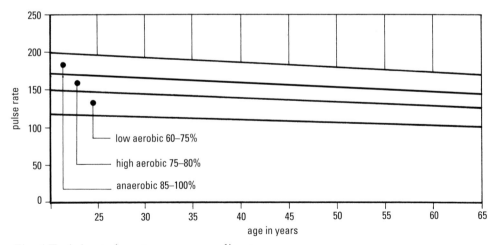

Fig. 4 Training pulse-rate ranges according to age.

CHAPTER 2

Advanced Aerobic Training

As an athlete improves, he or she will doubtless dream of competing at the dizzy heights of the Olympic games and even winning medals at this greatest of championships. Sebastian Coe, Steve Ovett and Kelly Holmes have all scaled the ultimate peak in endurance performance, achieving Olympic golds, while in their time Dave Bedford, Dave Moorcroft, Steve Cram and Paula Radcliffe have produced greater performances than anyone else in the world.

All these top runners started as beginners, moving up the scale of performance to reach the pinnacle. It is, however, no mistake that all had, or have, great coaches and made, or continue to make, use of all the methods and techniques available to them to achieve their success. It is in the area of assessing an athlete's needs and performance that the most important advances in coaching have been made, thus stimulating greater achievements and ever-faster times.

Over the last three decades, the nations that have consistently produced the best runners are those with natural and cultural advantages. Being born and living at altitude confers a massive advantage over runners based at sea-level, while an active early life involving running also has a major effect on a later ability to run. The recognition of these advantages has stimulated research into sea-level running in an attempt to even out the playing field, and some of the results produced have been particularly influential, especially on European athletes.

This chapter looks at the advanced and sophisticated measures of training effect that are now available to athletes. These are generally laboratory-based techniques, and include the measurement of maximum oxygen used during exercise (VO_2max), the threshold of exercise at which lactic acid rises markedly (onset of blood lactate, or OBL), the ratio of oxygen used to carbon dioxide produced (respiratory exchange ratio, or RER), and biomechanical running efficiency analysis.

VO_2MAX

The measurement of maximum oxygen used during exercise (VO_2max) was once thought to be the Holy Grail of endurance science. Every athlete was tested, and coaches used the results as a base indicator of whether an individual could carry out the training tasks necessary to attain world-class performance. Masses of information was accumulated, giving very accurate ranges for VO_2max for both members of the general public and athletes. Norms for men are 48–60ltr per minute, with male athletes reaching beyond 70ltr per minute at the top end of the scale. For women, these figures are slightly lower, with the norm at

40–50ltr per minute and elite performers at 65ltr or more per minute.

It has since been found that it is not the absolute value of VO_2max that matters in terms of ability and progress, but ultimately the efficiency of the runner in getting as close to this level as possible. In other words, two runners with near-identical VO_2max measurements may actually have very dissimilar running abilities. One may run very economically and therefore use more of his or her available oxygen towards this, while the other may use a higher proportion of the oxygen in useless muscular activity unrelated to the event. This is one very good reason why endurance athletes should focus on running technically well and as economically as possible, using few extraneous movements of uninvolved parts of the body.

Having said this, many coaches still use VO_2max as a training indicator and much work has been carried out on trying to find non-laboratory-based techniques for assessing the VO_2max base level and the efficiency of running. The problem with these techniques is that they all involve the use of calculations, which at best are a reflection of statistical norms and therefore by definition contain built-in errors. Such methods can therefore give only an indication of training effectiveness and the state of an athlete's aerobic ability, and as such are of limited use. (For more details on laboratory testing of VO_2max, *see* Chapter 9.)

This has not stopped the search for the ultimate track-based system for measuring running efficiency and ability. As good a measurement as any is the time it takes an individual to run 3,000m at an even speed, although this is little different from saying that the best indicator of ability is the time it takes the athlete to complete his or her chosen event. In other words, the personal best in competition shows the coach how good the training is. For more on VO_2max testing, *see* Chapter 9.

ONSET OF BLOOD LACTATE (OBL)

Since the late 1980s, sports scientists have focused on lactic acid as an indicator of when aerobic exercise moves into the anaerobic area – in other words, as the indicator of what level of training marks the limit of the aerobic system. Lactic acid is produced by the muscles when there is insufficient oxygen available to oxidize (burn) the body's energy sources (fats, carbohydrates and amino acids). It is poisonous to the body and increases the acidity of the blood, creating a range of debilitating effects. As it accumulates in the muscles, intercellular fluid and blood, pain is felt and the ability to move decreases severely. Basically, you poison yourself. (*See* Chapter 3 for more on lactic acid.)

There are three main ways in which lactic acid is removed from the muscles:

1. It can be removed by passing from the muscle into the intercellular fluid, and from there into the lymphatic system. This is slow and inefficient compared with the need to remove the substance.
2. It can pass from the intercellular fluid into the blood, and from there to the liver, where it is broken down. This is more effective in removing lactic acid from the system.
3. It can itself be used as an energy source to produce ATP. This is the most important means of removing lactic acid permanently.

The body uses all three methods on a continuous basis to try to reduce levels of lactic acid. When the processes are finally overwhelmed and a build-up of the substance occurs, physical activity becomes painful and finally halts altogether. The point at which the amount of lactic acid in the blood can no longer be removed and starts to accumulate is called the onset of blood lactate (OBL) and can be assessed by testing the blood during exercise.

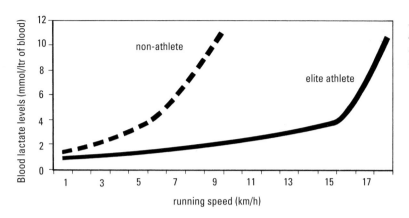

Fig. 5 Graph showing how blood lactate levels increase with exercise intensity.

This test and the protocol associated with it are further explained in Chapter 9.

Much of the early work on OBL in the UK was performed by top international cycling coach Peter Keen when he was working with the Olympic team. His results speak for themselves in that his protégé, Chris Boardman, gained Olympic gold and went on to become one of the world's best in the professional sport. Peter's work was initially based in the laboratory since portable testing equipment was not available to analyse samples on the track at the time. Subsequently, it has become available, and any athlete with serious international intentions now has regular OBL assessments.

Levels of blood lactic acid are normally below 1.5 millimoles per litre of blood (1.5mmol/ltr). When exercise occurs, this gradually increases as the effort increases in intensity and the various mechanisms to rid the system of the acid come into play. Initially, the increase is linear, and the point at which the increase occurs is called the aerobic threshold. At a concentration of around 4mmol/ltr, the system can no longer remove lactic acid effectively and the levels rise exponentially. This point is considered to be the OBL, or anaerobic threshold. The highest level to which the oxygen uptake can be pushed is the VO_2max.

Unfortunately, nature is not uniform and so the OBL is not as precise or as consistent as we would like it to be. It is for this reason that the average level of 4mmol/ltr has been chosen as the standard, and it is this that is used as a training indicator.

The graph above shows examples of blood lactic acid profiles for a non-athlete and an elite athlete. The non-athlete's levels of lactic acid move up immediately exercise starts and continue to rise inexorably, reaching the OBL threshold at a fairly low speed of running. In contrast, the profile of the elite athlete shows a much slower increase in lactic acid as running speed increases. At around 15km/h the OBL is reached and thereafter the blood lactic acid level increases rapidly.

The simple object of a training programme is to shift the graph to the right, meaning that an athlete will be able to run faster at a steady level without his or her blood lactic acid reaching performance-reducing amounts. If the heart rate is measured at the same time as running speed and lactic acid levels, the coach can easily calculate the heart-rate level and the speed at which the athlete needs to train in order to be working close to and above the OBL.

One of the essential pieces of apparatus that needs to be used during most training, therefore, is the radio heart-rate monitor. This

Athlete using a heart-rate monitor.

consists of a sensor mounted on chest band that transmits data to a wrist receiver. The recorded data can then be reviewed on the wrist receiver or downloaded onto a computer, where the results can be plotted graphically and analysed statistically away from the training venue. Using this technique, the whole session can be monitored and the training adjusted according to the results obtained. Clearly, this quick and effective method of training assessment provides considerable information to the coach, who needs accurate feedback in order to estimate the validity of the training programme. For more on OBL testing, *see* Chapter 9.

RESPIRATORY EXCHANGE RATIO (RER)

Measuring the ratio of carbon dioxide (CO_2) produced to the oxygen (O_2) used during exercise, which is called the respiratory exchange ratio (RER), is a useful indicator of what fuels are being burnt by the body. The test is mainly carried out in the laboratory setting, as the oxygen use and carbon dioxide production must be assessed accurately if a sufficiently good indicator of the ratio of the two is to be calculated. Generally accepted norms are given below:

- 0.5–0.6 CO_2/O_2 – mainly fats being used.
- 0.6–0.8 CO_2/O_2 – mixed fuels (fats, amino acids and some carbohydrates).
- 0.8–1.0 CO_2/O_2 – mainly carbohydrates being used.

These values are very significant to the endurance athlete, since they give an indication of what energy sources are being used at differing speeds of running. The closer to the VO_2max an athlete works, the more carbohydrate is burnt as measured by the RER. As the speed drops, the RER falls correspondingly and thus the fuel used changes toward a mixture of carbohydrates, amino acids and fats. The RER also changes according to how long the exercise is performed. As time moves on, the carbohydrate stores can start to deplete dramatically, with a concomitant decrease in RER indicating a move to fat burning.

Measuring the RER during a race can therefore give the coach and athlete an indication of any dramatic changes in energy source and so any potential points when either the performance might drop or an intake of certain foods might be of benefit. However, the difficulty of doing this is that for the RER to be measured, assessments of oxygen and carbon dioxide levels must be made, something that can be done accurately only in the laboratory. Running for 2½ hours on a treadmill is not easy, particularly with a sensor-loaded mouthpiece in place. This difficulty accounts for the singular lack of statistics in this field. Most studies have been performed on a much shorter timescale than the duration of an endurance race, so the information is of only marginal use.

BIOMECHANICAL RUNNING EFFICIENCY ANALYSIS

Running efficiency is clearly the target for all serious athletes competing in endurance events. The greater the efficiency, the greater the economy of running and the better the athlete is able to utilize the limited resources of his or her body.

Probably the best example of the difference between efficient and inefficient running is in the use of the arms – exaggerated arm actions in endurance events lead to wasted energy. Similarly, excess movements of the body and head can both also reduce efficiency. The ideal runner performs the minimum of extraneous muscular actions, introducing necessary increases only as required for acceleration or other manoeuvres.

Seeing Haile Gebrselassie run is like watching poetry in motion, as he uses minimum movements to produce maximum effectiveness. In contrast, Paula Radcliffe apparently has several inefficient movement patterns, but compared with her earlier action she has made massive improvements and has reached a balanced and effective style of running.

Initially, the best way to assess a runner is by observation. This requires a good coaching eye and patience, as most runners start off with many problems. It is only by constant correction and change that the runner will reach his or her optimum, if not a perfect running action. The more subtle inefficiencies can be highlighted only through biomechanical analysis using video, pressure-platform work and foot-placement profile analysis, all of which are restricted to the biomechanics laboratory. These more sophisticated techniques are additional to the visual analysis of the coach and can help if there is problem that is not obvious to the naked eye.

When making changes in running action, it is useful to assess their effect on pulse rate at the same time for a set piece of work. This standard comparison is a simple way of checking whether the changes really are effective, but it must be said that any change needs to be ingrained by much repetition before efficiency improvements become obvious. In order to achieve ultimate success it is vital that such difficult and time-consuming changes are made and are integrated fully into the everyday running action.

Running action is also closely related to footwear. Many athletes assume that paying a lot of money for the latest style of shoe will automatically be a progressive step. In truth, this is usually not the case, since the shape of an individual's feet, the position of the arches and the actual size of each foot (they often differ) are all variables that need addressing if the footwear is to help rather than hinder the running action. It is therefore obvious that individualized footwear will be of far greater benefit to runners, helping reduce injury and fatigue in the legs.

Most advanced shoe retailers are now able to profile athletes' feet, and can recommend the correct footwear for both training and competition. Such shoes will fit perfectly and will provide the correct support in the correct place, keeping the feet in a balanced and neutral position at all times. If in doubt, athletes should consult an expert or at the very least try out several pairs of shoes to find the best and most comfortable fit.

SUMMARY

- Advances in endurance science have enabled athletes to train in a more sophisticated and effective way. Methods of assessing performance and training effectiveness have both played an important role in tuning training regimes to meet the real needs of athletes.
- Paying attention to detail has increased the ability of the coach to make the judgements necessary to speed up improvement and reduce racing times. This is not to say, however, that the basics of endurance training have become easier – hard work is still the basis for achieving the ultimate goals. While science does play its part, highly motivated effort continues to lie at the heart of success.

CHAPTER 3

General Anaerobic Conditioning

The use of resistance training has been developed over many years to improve athletes' anaerobic abilities. It particularly applies to endurance runners, as tolerating the results of anaerobic running is part and parcel of their sport.

Every road-runner knows that races are won or lost on hills. The ability to cope with such adverse terrain must therefore be part of every endurance runner's arsenal of abilities. All endurance athletes, from the 800m runner to the marathoner, can benefit from practising on hills or performing other resistance activities, as it is only through the use of such strategies that the ability to tolerate the pain involved with anaerobic running can be achieved.

Unfortunately, pain is the basis of high-quality anaerobic training. Tolerance to a high level of lactic acid in the body is essential to improving performance under anaerobic duress. Every runner will understand how high levels of lactic acid can reduce the ability to move to virtually zero, and how trying to carry on in such a situation can be extremely painful and even lead to vomiting. It is essential, however, that the serious athlete pushes him or herself to this extreme, if only to feel what effect such training has on the body as a whole.

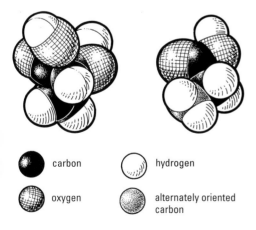

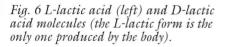

carbon

hydrogen

oxygen

alternately oriented carbon

Fig. 6 L-lactic acid (left) and D-lactic acid molecules (the L-lactic form is the only one produced by the body).

WHAT IS LACTIC ACID?

Lactic acid is produced during the formation of ATP from pyruvic acid (a breakdown product of glucose) when little or no oxygen is available for aerobic respiration. Although the process is inefficient, it enables the last gasp of physical activity to take place when the athlete has run out of options. Production of lactic acid also has its cost.

Lactic acid is a simple chemical (2-hydroxy-propanoic acid, or $C_3H_6O_3$) that is soluble in water and has a strong acidic characteristic.

21

The fluids in the body can tolerate quite high concentrations of lactic acid by counteracting its acidity with buffers. These are chemicals that can absorb the hydrogen ions that are created by the presence of acids, thus effectively neutralizing them and their effects. The blood itself is slightly alkaline and must be maintained at this level for the body's fluid and chemical balance to be sustained within normal levels. Rising lactic acid levels can be counteracted up to a concentration of around 3–5mmol/ltr. At this point, the body's buffers are exhausted and the acidity of the blood and other fluids rises rapidly. This changes how the fluids and chemicals travel around the body and between tissues, thus fundamentally altering the whole metabolism in a negative way. The athlete is well aware when this point is reached, since any physical activity becomes difficult and painful.

Rest or a drastic slowing down are the only ways to alleviate the situation. When the high-level activity ceases, lactic acid can be removed from the system by being converted back into pyruvic acid and hence more ATP. It can also be removed by the liver, which again converts it into pyruvic acid and thence into glucose, a pathway that requires oxygen. This is the basis of the oxygen debt, which causes the puffing and blowing that continues even when exercise has ceased in order to restore body systems to normal. Gradually, the lactic acid is broken down and disperses, the pain goes and the ability to exercise returns.

For athletes, particularly those competing in the shorter endurance events (800m and 1,500m), tolerance to lactic acid is essential. By training at a high level, this tolerance can be built up. Such effort also increases the body's ability to deal with the offending chemical by improving the pathways that remove it from the system. Speed endurance, strength endurance and resistance running, particularly up hills, are especially effective methods for achieving this tolerance, because the level of lactic acid can be controlled by the extensivity and intensity of the sessions. Such work should start slowly so that the athlete can prepare mentally for what will be very hard sessions both physically or psychologically.

RUNNING-BASED ANAEROBIC CONDITIONING

Interval Running

This type of training is at the heart of most short-endurance runners' programmes. It is the domain of the specialist endurance coach and so is not dealt with in any detail here, suffice it to say that the performance of interval training is the most effective way to improve tolerance to, and bodily handling of, lactic acid.

An inexhaustible variety of sessions can be used, but the basic principle is that an intense run is followed by a period of rest or lower-level activity. For middle-distance runners, this ratio should be around one period of exercise to 1.5 periods of rest, while runners training for longer-endurance events should aim for one period of running to one of rest. These ratios are reflected in the different energy sources used in the different events.

Hill Running (Strength Endurance)

Hill running is perhaps the easiest type of training to achieve the required effect, since the surroundings can be pleasant and the athlete is not just focusing on the normal environment of the track. For this reason, the coach should choose a venue that provides an uplifting effect.

Again, an infinite number of sessions can be performed, from short, very fast uphill runs to efforts sustained over a longer period. The key is to maintain a high level of activity, using about a third of full recovery time between

Hill runners.
(COURTESY OF
WEBSHOTS.COM)

3 × 100m fast stride
At 90 per cent effort; jog back recovery.

3 × 150m fast stride
At 85 per cent effort; jog back recovery.

3 × 100m fast stride
At 90 per cent effort; jog back recovery.

3 × 50m sprint
At 100 per cent effort; jog back recovery.

If possible, the athlete's performance should be recorded, not only in terms of times but also using a radio pulse monitor. This will allow the coach to check the severity of the sessions and their effectiveness. Monitoring any session must be part of the coach's work, as it is only by doing this that the efficacy of the training can be assessed.

The Southampton-based international track coach Mike Smith, who worked with Roger Black and Kriss Akabusi, among many others, in the 1980s and 1990s, used hill running as a central plank of his winter training programmes. His squad knew that hill days were going to be hard, but they produced the best results ever recorded in the UK. Variations on hill running include the use of sand dunes, which was a method favoured by the famous Australian coach Percy Cerutti when training Herb Elliott, who achieved the 1,500m world record and a gold medal at the 1960 Rome Olympics. Indeed, hill running on a variety of terrains has been used to improve the general anaerobic conditioning of athletes for many years, not least because it is so simple and effective.

repetitions so that the lactic acid continues to build after each repetition. The pulse-rate decline profile after flat-out running should be tested at the start of the programme to ascertain the full-recovery time for the athlete. This will change as the athlete improves his or her aerobic and anaerobic fitness, and so will need to be retested at regular intervals.

Coaches should be careful with this form of training, as lactic acid tolerance varies greatly between athletes, and they should never be pushed over the edge of acceptability. Train very hard, yes; train to destruction, no. Some athletes never know when to quit, and the coach must be the judge of when enough is enough. A typical hill session, conducted on a 15- to 20-degree incline, could consist of the following for a mature athlete:

3 × 50m sprint
At 100 per cent effort; jog back recovery (timed to make sure the right level of recovery has been achieved).

Speed Endurance

This form of track conditioning is usually used specifically by sprinters to enable them to minimize the slowing down that occurs at the end of their races. It consists of running sessions in which the athlete trains as near to maximal speed as possible but with less than adequate recovery between repetitions. For example, if an athlete takes ten minutes to recover fully from a flat-out 150m sprint, a session consisting of five similar-distance runs with three minutes of recovery between each would induce a high level of lactic acid towards the end. There are innumerable variations on this type of session, but the principle is the same: they should be fast, with little recovery. The athlete will soon learn how hard anaerobic running is, and his or her body will start to adapt to the stress.

This type of session is excellent for anaerobically conditioning all types of endurance athlete, but it must be remembered that long-distance athletes do not have a high proportion of fast-twitch fibres and will therefore need to perform longer-distance runs and have less recovery time than shorter-distance athletes. The correct level of effort should be ascertained by recording the times of the runs together with the pulse-rate data during the sessions. The target pulse rate at the end of each run should be between 170 and 200 for a 20- to 25-year-old athlete. Long-distance athletes may find it very hard to achieve this, but should strive to reach as near this level as possible.

Resistance Running

This is another very useful method for working in the anaerobic range. It entails running on the flat against a resistance applied either by another person or a weight of some description, such as a tyre or weight disc. The resistance is attached via a harness, preferably one made for the purpose to spread the force throughout the torso of the athlete. It is not advisable for the force to pull only on the hips, as this will cause the athlete to adopt an unnatural running posture. Additionally, it is much better to have only a moderate resisting force, as too great a resistance also causes changes to the running position.

The runs should be 50–100m in length, followed by less than adequate recovery periods. Again, times and pulse rates should be monitored to check that the training is within the correct range of difficulty.

It should be noted that resistance running is a very strenuous form of activity and so must be restricted to athletes who are fully fit and have good control over their running technique (any imbalance in technique will be exaggerated during this activity). The Achilles tendons are a particular area of concern, as the athlete must lean forward slightly to work against the resistance – if his or her tendons are short or damaged, they will come under severe extra strain.

Water Running

Strictly speaking, resistance running while fully immersed in water and using a flotation jacket is primarily a rehabilitation method employed during periods when running is impossible, as the full running movement can be performed without any impact strain. By its very nature, this type of conditioning does not work the calves and ankles, but all other running muscles and joints can effectively be trained in this way.

Water running can also be a very effective anaerobic (as well as aerobic) activity, which as a bonus will have little negative effect on any of the joints or muscle–tendon units. The key is to wear the correct flotation vest – this must enable the athlete to float comfortably in the water without any effort on his or her part. Repetition training can then be performed in a similar way to that on hills or on the track. Using the same speed/recovery parameters as the other forms of anaerobic conditioning will produce effective results and add a very different aspect to what is normally hard, tedious training.

Flotation jacket.

GENERAL GYM-BASED CONDITIONING (STRENGTH ENDURANCE

Chapter 7 describes how gymnasium exercises can be used to work on weaknesses in the body. Such sessions can, however, also be used as a general method for both aerobic and anaerobic conditioning.

Circuit training and body-weight stage training can either be aerobic or anaerobic in their effect, depending on how fast the exercises are performed, what combination is used and the intensity at which they are performed. Clearly, the same parameters in terms of pulse rate and recovery between exercises as used with other training methods must be adhered

to, in order to ensure the correct effect. Thus, the desired results will be achieved if, at the end of each exercise set, the pulse can be kept at the 170–200 mark for anaerobic conditioning, or at the 130–150 mark for aerobic conditioning, and allowed to drop slightly during the recovery between sets.

For a more general effect, the exercises should be less muscularly specific. Examples of general circuit and body-weight stage training sessions are shown below. These will have a more general anaerobic effect when performed with high intensity and a more general aerobic effect when performed at a less intense level. Care must be taken to train at the right intensity to achieve the desired result.

General Circuit Training

A circuit consists of a range of exercises performed as a continuous series, with the athlete returning to the first exercise only when one whole set of each of the other exercises has been completed. The important point is that there is *no recovery* between exercises or circuits. When the final exercise has been reached, the whole circuit is started again. Because the athlete returns to an exercise only when he or she has completed all the others, the focus is taken off the different muscle groups in turn. Circuits therefore have a more general effect than stage training, when all the sets of one exercise are performed before the next is started. Both forms of training are, however, very effective in terms of general anaerobic conditioning if they are performed at the correct intensity.

To ensure that the circuit has a general effect, the exercises themselves must be general in nature, employing as many muscle groups as possible each time. The session must be performed at such a pace as to maintain the pulse rate described above. As with running or cycling, the faster the activity is performed, the greater the anaerobic element involved.

Sample Circuit

This circuit should be performed four times for the first session, five for the second and six for the third and subsequent sessions, when it should be timed. For best effect the exercises must be performed in the order stated. The numbers following the name of each exercise indicate the number of repetitions – for example, '10' means ten repetitions should be done, while '8/8' indicates that eight repetitions should be performed on the right side followed by eight on the left.

Squat thrusts – 10

When performed properly, this time-honoured exercise which is most effective in working the whole body and, more specifically, the hip flexors and rectus abdominis muscles. To execute the correct movement, the athlete starts in a strict press-up position, the body being held in line with the legs (the hips should not sag). From here, the legs are flexed and the knees brought towards the arms and tucked just inside the elbows. The feet are lifted off the ground to achieve a clean movement. The return to the start position is achieved by reversing this movement. It is vital that the exercise is completed and performed correctly to obtain the best effect.

Chinnies – 8/8

This is another exercise for the rectus abdominis, hip flexors, obliques and transversus muscles. Unlike sit-ups and sit-backs, it is more dynamic and requires more skill to perform properly.

The athlete lies on his or her back, with legs outstretched and the fingers touching the ears. One knee is raised towards the shoulders and, at the same time, the body is curled up to the point where the elbow moves outside

the opposite knee. It is vital that the full range is used, as the exercise becomes progressively less effective the shorter the range. The body is then lowered to the start position with legs outstretched. The movement is repeated, except the opposite knee is raised and the other elbow pushed outside. Once the basic movement has been mastered, the whole exercise can be performed with rhythm, although accuracy of performance must not be sacrificed for speed.

Full-arm body circling – 8/8

Standing full-arm body circling is not normally used in circuits, even though it is an excellent exercise for conditioning the mid-region muscles. It is performed by standing with the feet well astride. The arms are extended and then swept round in a circle, touching the ground in the forward low position and up as far as possible in the upright position. The movement should be as extensively ranged and as loose as possible, and should be performed smoothly. All the repetitions are completed in one direction, after which they are carried out in the opposite direction.

Narrow-stance alternate-leg split jumps – 8/8

This is a variation on standard squat jumps. The feet are placed narrowly apart at the start, with one back and one forward. The athlete then bends fully and jumps. While he or she is in mid-air, the feet are exchanged so that they are split the opposite way on landing.

This is an excellent exercise for all athletic events, as it uses the more natural position of one foot forward and one foot back, thus relating more closely to athletic activities. Working each leg independently also introduces significant balance and posture elements that do not occur in the normal squat jump.

Squat thrusts.

Chinnies.

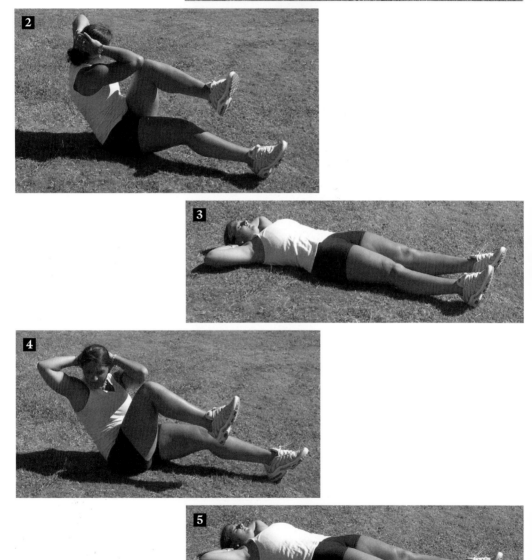

Full-arm body circling.

Narrow-stance alternate-leg split jumps.

Alternate-leg 'V' sits – 8/8

In alternate-leg 'V' sits, the athlete starts off by lying flat on the floor on his or her back, with the arms extended and touching the ground above the head. From here, one leg is raised and the body curled up so that the hands reach for and touch the toes of the raised foot. The starting position is then resumed, and the other leg is raised and the toes touched. This is repeated smoothly so that a rhythm is set up. It is vital that the toes and not the ankles are touched, otherwise the movements will be shortened and so will be less effective.

Feet-raised bench dips – 10

This is an easy version of normal dips. The body is suspended between two chairs or benches (make sure these are stable, or hold them in position), facing upwards and supported by the hands (with arms locked straight) and the heels. The elbows are then bent so that the backside moves towards the ground and touches it. At this point the arms are extended to push the body back up to the starting position.

The exercise works the anterior deltoids and the triceps. It also uses the full backward range of the shoulder and is therefore beneficial in maintaining or improving this. It is important not to sacrifice range for speed.

Full squat jumps – 10

Squat jumps are one of the simplest and best exercises for the legs, but they are also one of the worst performed in terms of technique. The object is to bend the legs fully and then jump vertically as high as possible. On landing, the legs are bent to absorb the shock and to prepare for the next repetition. The jumps should be performed continuously.

Problems come when the athlete finds the jumps difficult to perform owing to a lack of suppleness or because he or she is simply too weak to start with. In these cases, the legs are not bent but instead the body is piked forward, putting considerable strain on the lower back and doing very little for the legs. If the athlete is stiff in the ankles or the Achilles tendons, similar problems may also arise. It is therefore very important to teach the exercise well, making sure the head is held up, the hands touch the ears, the elbows are kept in to the side, and the back is as near vertical and as straight as possible. This can take some time, but the benefits of correct performance are considerable.

Free twisting hyperextensions – 6/6

This exercise works the lower back in a rotational fashion and is performed by lying on the front, with the hands held behind the ears. From here, the back is arched backwards and one shoulder twisted to the side; this position is then held for two seconds. The start position is resumed and the next repetition is initiated with a twist to the other side. The movement should be performed smoothly; any jerking into position may cause cramping.

Free twisting sit-ups – 8/8

Sit-ups performed with no support of the feet (free sit-ups) are quite difficult for beginners. If the athlete finds them impossible to do, the feet can be secured to start with, although a much better effect will be achieved if this is not done.

The athlete lies on the ground with the knees bent at about thirty degrees and the body flat. The hands are placed across the upper chest and held there firmly (they must never be placed behind the neck, as this can damage the small neck vertebrae if undue pressure is exerted). From here, the body is curled up so that the head meets the knees, after which it is lowered to the starting position.

31

Alternate-leg 'V' sits.

Feet-raised bench dips.

THIS PAGE:
Full squat jumps.

OPPOSITE PAGE:
Free twisting hyperextensions.

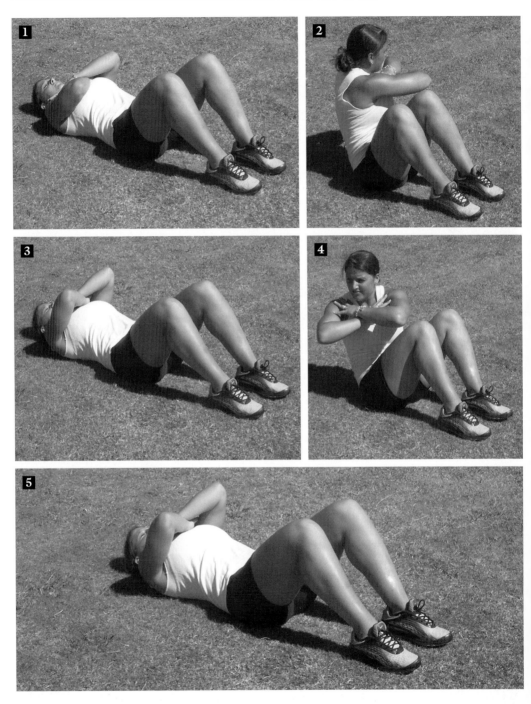

THIS PAGE: *Free twisting sit-ups.*   OPPOSITE PAGE: *Supported bounce jumps.*

On the second repetition, the body is rotated to one side as it rises. The third repetition is rotated to the other side, after which the sequence is repeated. These rotations ensure that the oblique and transverse abdominal muscles are worked in addition to the rectus abdominis.

This exercise is difficult and can be painful for athletes who have back problems. In this case, sit-backs are safer. These are performed by starting in a sitting position with the knees bent and the arms crossed over the chest. From here, the body is lowered to the point where only the lower back touches the ground, after which it is returned to the starting position. This ensures that the back is never overextended and so should not cause damage to the lumbar vertebrae. If in doubt, avoid the exercise altogether.

Supported bounce jumps – 25

This is a simple, safe and effective plyometric exercise. It is performed by standing upright, close to some wall bars or other supporting structure such as a dipping bar. The hands are lightly placed on the support and, after a shallow leg dip, the athlete jumps as high as possible with additional upward push being supplied by the arms. This lifts the athlete higher than could be achieved by using the legs alone and therefore creates a more forceful drop to the ground. The object is then to bounce immediately on landing and again jump as high as possible.

The emphasis is thus both on jumping high and on reacting quickly on hitting the ground, the whole action being moderated by the supporting arm action. Note that the arms must not be used except for support and to provide slight lift at the end of the leg drive.

General Body-weight Stage Training

As mentioned earlier, stage training entails performing a series of exercises similar to those used for a circuit, but in such a way that all the sets of one exercise are completed before the next is commenced. This makes the session harder in many ways, as one group of muscles is exhausted and this tiredness then has to be carried through to the next exercise set. Although lactic acid tends to build more locally than in a circuit, the method is still an excellent means of conditioning the body anaerobically.

The sample session on the following pages uses a number of very general exercises and thus varies from the sessions described in Chapter 7, which are designed to focus on weak areas. The session is performed by completing all four sets of the first exercise, followed by all four sets of the second and so on, until it has been completed. The pulse rate can be allowed to go as high as is tolerable and should be pushed to its limit. Recovery should be in the region of fifteen to thirty seconds between each set and thirty seconds between exercises that must be timed and adhered to accurately.

Sample Session

Burpees – 4 × 10

Burpees are a combination of a squat thrust followed by full star jump. It is vital for the effectiveness of the exercise that both the squat thrust and the star jump are performed properly – beware, as sometimes they degenerate to little more than a shuffle followed by shallow jump.

The squat thrust must be performed from the full press-up, extended-body start position to a final position where the knees are tucked between the arms. The star jump must then be a complete jump, with arms and legs extended in a star shape, the body vertical and the head up. It is important to establish a rhythm for this exercise as this makes it much easier to perform well.

Burpees.

Press-ups (full range).

Press-ups (full range) – 4 × 8

The press-up is another classic exercise. It mainly strengthens the anterior deltoids, triceps and pectoral muscles, with additional work on the mid-region, particularly the rectus abdominis muscles. It is performed correctly by lying on the floor with the hands at either side of the shoulders. The body is held rigid and the arms push it up until they are fully extended. There should be no sag in the mid-region and, when the body is lowered again, it should reach the ground as one unit, with the hips and chest touching simultaneously.

Alternate-leg reverse raises – 4 × 10/10

This exercise is excellent for core stability in the back. The start position sees the athlete lying face-down with the hands tucked under the chin. From here, each leg is raised straight up and held for three seconds before it is lowered to the ground again. The other leg is then raised, held and lowered.

It is most important that the hips are not twisted in order to raise the leg higher. If the hips are too stiff to allow an effective range of movement, more suppling work should be carried out to correct the problem.

Narrow-stance alternate bounce jumps for height – 4 × 10/10

This exercise has a twofold effect in that it works the calves isotonically (with normal concentric/eccentric contractions) but also encourages a reactive (plyometric) response from the muscles when performed well. At the start, the feet are in a toe-to-heel position and the body is upright, with the hands held loosely behind the ears. The eyes are focused upwards throughout the duration of the exercise. From here, the knees are bent slightly and then immediately straightened to create a powerful jump for height. During the jump, the feet exchange positions. The next repetition is performed as reactively as possible, but still aiming for maximum elevation. Rhythm helps in the performance of the exercise.

'V' sits – 4 × 10

'V' sits require coordination, but this improves with repetition. The athlete lies flat on the floor on his or her back, with the legs and arms outstretched and touching the ground. From here, both hands are raised and at the same time the legs are lifted. The object is to touch both hands on both feet by raising the arms and legs simultaneously into a 'V' position, and then returning to the starting point. It is important that each repetition is completed fully; if not, the beneficial effect of the exercise is dramatically reduced.

Knee-tuck jumps – 4 × 15

Some people find this simple exercise very difficult to perform and so require practice before they get it right. It is, however, worth persevering with it and even doing extra practice in order to perform it well, as it is an excellent conditioner of the hip flexors, an area of the mid-region that is weak in many endurance athletes.

The exercise entails a powerful two-footed jump, with the knees pulled up to (or near) the chest during the off-ground time. The feet are then returned to the ground and the next repetition is commenced immediately to create a vigorous, continuous rhythm.

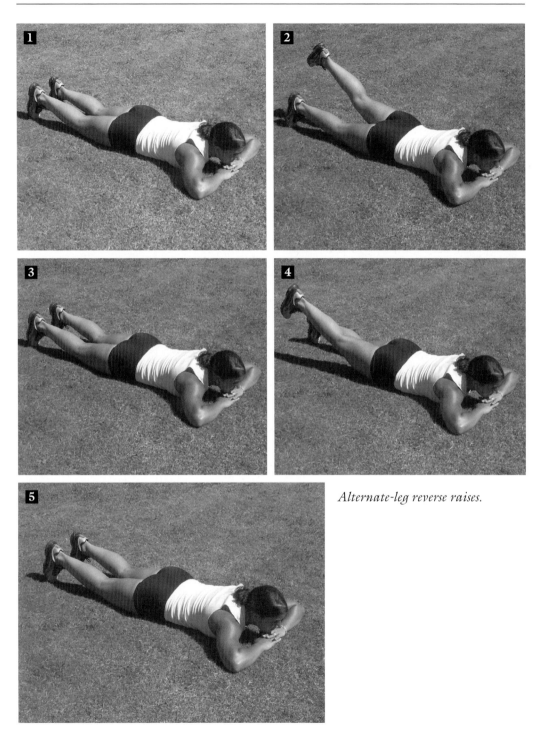

Alternate-leg reverse raises.

Narrow-stance alternate bounce jumps for height.

43

'V' sits.

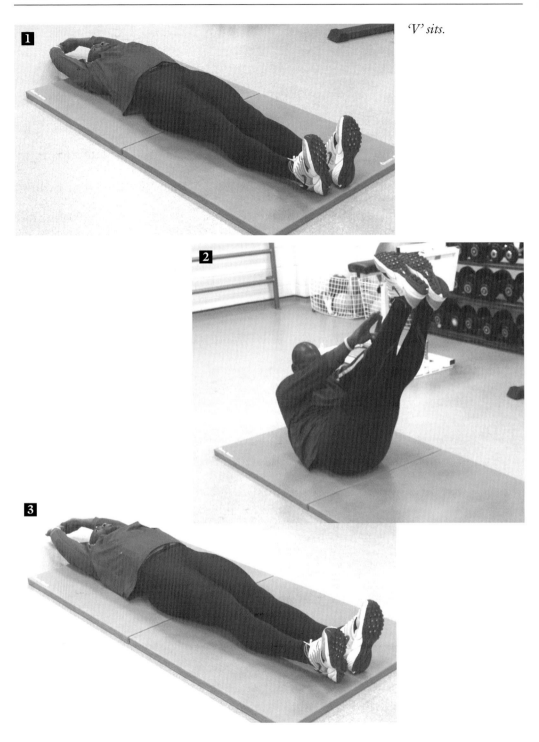

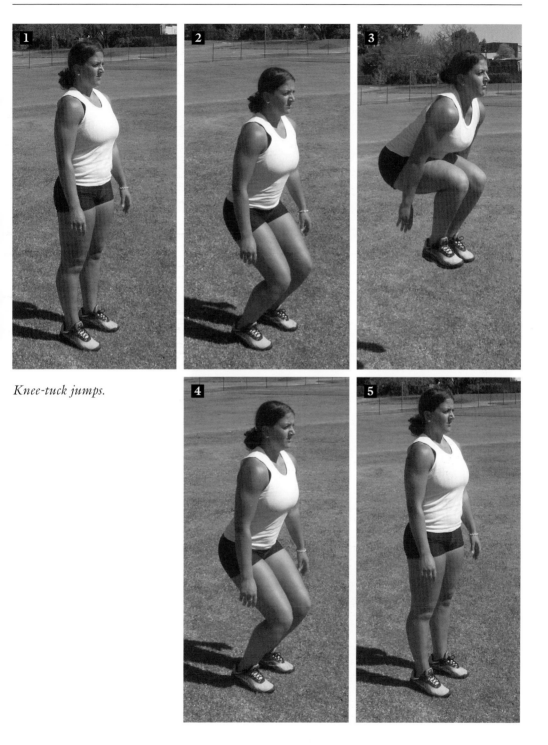

Knee-tuck jumps.

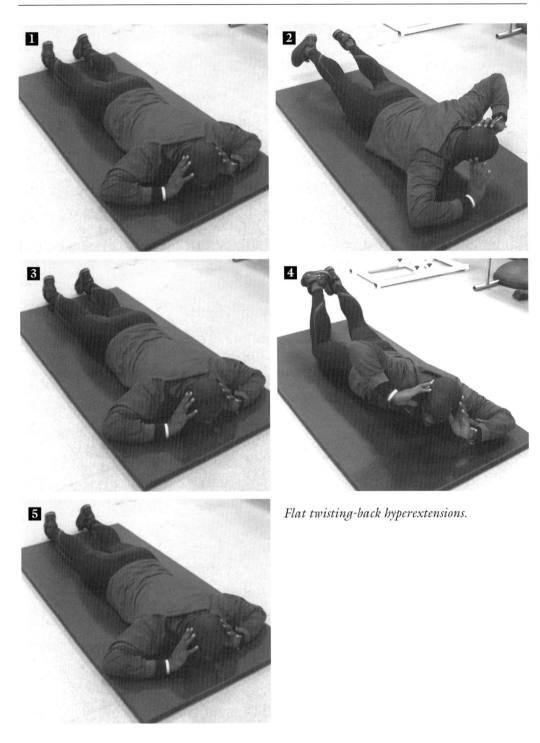

Flat twisting-back hyperextensions.

Flat twisting-back hyperextensions – 4 × 8/8

This exercise works the lower back in a rotational fashion and is performed by lying on the front with the hands held behind the ears. From here, the back is arched backwards and one shoulder is twisted to the side; this position is held for three seconds. The start position is then resumed and the next repetition is initiated with a twist to the other side. The movement should be performed smoothly, as any jerking may cause cramping.

Body-upright lunges – 4 × 8/8

Body-upright lunges are performed by starting in feet-together standing position with the hands held lightly behind the ears (they must remain here throughout the exercise). From here, a long step forward is taken, with the body kept vertical. Once the athlete is in this extended position, the front leg is driven strongly to push him or her back to the start position. There should be as little sag as possible, and a firm, dynamic movement that is fast and well balanced should be the aim. When the starting position is resumed, the other leg is taken forward and the drive is repeated.

Athletes quite often have problems stretching out a long way and then driving sufficiently hard. This is something that can be worked on, but it is important that range of movement is as long as possible right from the word go.

Hip raises – 4 × 10

At first glance, hip raises appear easy to perform. However, the exercise uses many of the core stabilizing muscles of the gluteal group, as well as the lower back and hamstrings, and initially many athletes find it hard to perform well.

The athlete lies on his or her back with the knees very slightly bent, the elbows tucked into the side and the hands relaxed on the chest. From here, force is applied through the heels and shoulders so that the backside is lifted well clear of the ground. Once at maximum height, the body is held in position for three seconds (this period can be extended depending on how hard the athlete needs to work this area of the body). After this, the hips are lowered slowly to the starting position.

Alternate-leg step-in step-up drives – 4 × 10/10

This exercise combines a shallow lunge with a step-up drive and requires good coordination and skill. It is performed by starting in a standing position, feet together, and then stepping forward into the shallow lunge position. This is followed by an upward drive onto the toes, with the rear leg and arms finishing in the basic long-jump take-off position.

This is another good all-round exercise that helps to develop posture and stability during athletic movements. An alternative is to step up onto a bench and then perform the drive (bench step-up drives).

Both the circuit training session and bodyweight stage training session above are general in nature and will have an overall beneficial effect. If, as is usual, the athlete has imbalances in his or her conditioning, these will be exposed by performing these types of schedule. Having found the weaknesses, the coach can then design specific sessions to help rebalance the body. Examples of such sessions are discussed in Chapter 7.

THIS PAGE:
Body-upright lunges.

OPPOSITE PAGE:
Hip raises.

Alternate-leg step-in step-up drives.

SUMMARY

• Anaerobic conditioning is essential for endurance athletes as it not only increases lactic acid tolerance but also helps with the uphill running and accelerations that are sometimes needed in racing. Using various techniques to suit the athlete and the anticipated conditions of the event will enhance performance significantly.

• As they are alternative training methods, most anaerobic sessions can help relieve the boredom of repetitious steady work (which makes up much of an endurance athlete's schedule). The gymnasium can be the focus for as much of this conditioning as the track or hills, so long as it is carried out properly.

CHAPTER 4

The Importance of Running Technique and Posture

When you consider the huge number of near-identical movements an endurance athlete makes during training and in competition, it is hardly surprising that repetitive strain injuries are common. The body tends to react against repetitive movements by gradually becoming inflamed in stress points. For the runner, the

Relaxed running posture.
(COURTESY OF WEBSHOTS.COM)

Achilles tendon, knees and lower back are the key damage areas, and, in the longer term, the hip joints also show signs of wear and tear.

Conditioning the body to minimize this type of damage is an essential part of every serious endurance athlete's programme, even though some may not enjoy this aspect of training. It is very rare for endurance athletes to last many years at the top level of their sport without having established sound posture. In recent years, we have even seen marathoners running in the style of middle-distance runners and 10,000m-runners completing the last laps of their races like sprinters. In years gone by, it was rare to see such athletic ability in these events, which instead were generally the domain of the 'fast plodder' rather than the true runner. This is, of course, not decrying earlier athletes, but has merely been used as an example to point out that today, in order to win a long-distance race, athletes need to be able to run very fast for sustained periods and then have enough left to cap it off with a sprint finish.

Paula Radcliffe is a prime example of such an athlete, and is wonderful to see in full flight. Even though she has never been one of the world's most graceful runners, she more than makes up for this in excellent conditioning and a constant, powerful stride that makes maximum use of her strengths. Haile Gebrselassie, on the other hand, has immaculate running technique and appears to have no power at all until he takes off in the final stages of a race. Both his technique and posture are so good that he appears to float around the track, before pulling out unseen resources to sprint the rest. The Ethiopian has set the standards for those who are now following in his footsteps, showing the way to new levels of technical and physical performance despite his small, apparently frail frame.

Both these runners have different attributes, but both have achieved the ultimate in their events, proving that there are many ways to achieve greatness. However, underpinning every success is the athlete's ability to work at weaknesses in order to produce a chain of maximum strength.

A coach teaching good running posture.

POSTURE

It cannot be stressed too strongly how important balance and good technique are to running. Both the athlete and the coach must aim for the best postural, most economic running technique that can achieved. By doing this, the risk that injury will occur through the repetition of bad movements will be minimized. In addition, the energy needed for moving across the ground will be decreased, as less energy will be wasted in continually trying to bring the body back into balance as a result of bad technique.

I remember, as a child, my parents telling me not to slouch around or I would end up bent over double when I grew up. This made me aware at an early age that posture is important. I did not, of course, understand why this is so until later in life, but that early insistence by my parents gave me a lead on many of my fellow schoolchildren when it came to sport.

Virtually every physical activity is easier to perform if you have good posture, because this attribute means that you are setting the body up for such activity in the best possible way. For example, if you have a forward-curving spine as your normal posture, it will very difficult for you to run effectively as the curve will reduce your ability to use your hamstrings and gluteal muscles when trying to drive behind your body. Corrective conditioning must therefore be performed to improve posture and hence ensure the best possible running action. Ideally, young athletes should be taught the elements of basic posture and the correct techniques of walking, running and sprinting. If this happens, there will be few problems in later years when trying to enhance their ability to run.

Standing and Walking Drills

The simplest postural exercise is to stand erect and then balance a sizeable book on the head. Once it is firmly balanced, the basic activity of

ABOVE LEFT: Book on head – standing.
ABOVE RIGHT: Book on head – standing on one leg, high knee, hands straight out in front.

RIGHT: Book on head – walking.

walking without allowing the book to fall will help to generate excellent posture. Note that with all postural exercises many repetitions are needed to ingrain the positions and to train the muscles that are activated to create those positions.

Variations on the simple practice of standing and walking with a book on the head can be developed to make the activity more demanding. Examples are given below:

1. Standing, with arms by the side and concentrating on perfect upright posture.
2. Walking in a straight line holding the above posture.
3. Walking in curves, circles or figures of eight.
4. Standing on one leg, the free knee level with the hips and the arms held level with the shoulders.
5. Standing on one leg, the free knee level with the hips and the arms held down by the sides.

Book on head – standing on one leg, high knee, hands down by sides.

6. Standing on one leg, the free leg held out straight, level with hips, and the arms held level with the shoulders.
7. Standing on one leg, the free leg held out straight, level with hips, and the arms held down by the sides.

Exercises to improve posture without balancing a book on the head include the following:

1. Walking with exaggerated knee lifts but without allowing the hips to rotate forward (i.e. in a slumped position).
2. Zigzag running (one foot moves across in front of the other), backwards and forwards, holding the hips in the correct position.
3. Square-stepping – standing in the centre of a metre-diameter square and randomly stepping to the points of the square, both forward and backward.
4. Walking backwards, picking the heels up to the backside and keeping the hips in a firmly fixed position.

FAR LEFT: Book on head – standing on one leg, high leg, hands straight out in front.

LEFT: Book on head – standing on one leg, high leg, hands down by sides.

Walking with exaggerated knee lifts.

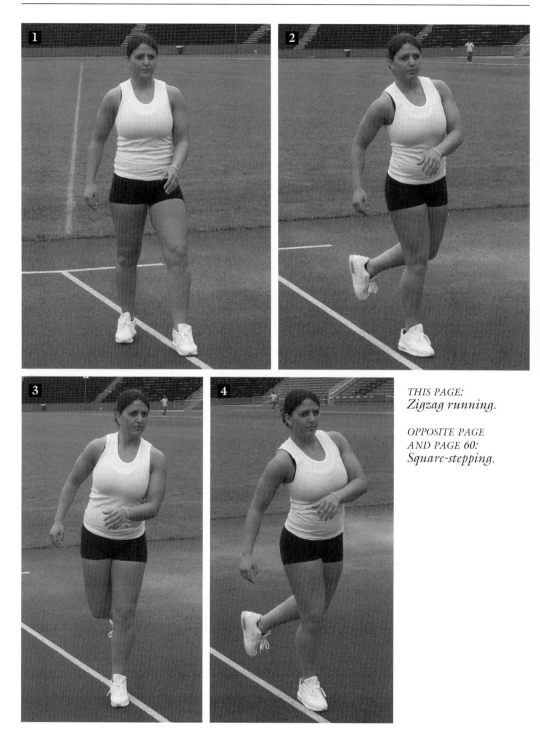

THIS PAGE:
Zigzag running.

OPPOSITE PAGE
AND PAGE 60:
Square-stepping.

THIS PAGE:
Square-stepping
(continued).

OPPOSITE PAGE:
Walking backwards.

Good running technique.

5. Steady running, working on correct posture as learnt during earlier sessions and making sure the arms are relaxed and are held at an optimal angle close to the body.

The above exercises will improve the posture of any runner, which in turn will reduce the potential for injury due to overstressing one or more parts of the supporting (core) structure of the mid-region and back. Each exercise should be performed for about three to five minutes, and a selection should be chosen to create a twenty- to thirty-minute session.

Running and Sprinting Drills

Running drills are activities in which one particular element of the running action is exaggerated. They are easy to do badly but are hard to perform well. Some simple examples are described below:

High-knee-lift running – 30m

This is performed by running steadily forward, bringing the lead knee up to the level of the hips. When the knee is at this level, the foot should be vertically underneath it and in a relaxed position. In addition, as the knee is lifted the hips must not be allowed to rotate up towards the knee. This is a simple test of the suppleness of the athlete's hamstrings and gluteal muscles. If the desired position cannot be achieved, urgent attention needs to be placed on correcting this lack of range.

High-knee-lift running.

Foot-flick-back running – 30m

Again, the athlete runs steadily forward, but this time the heels are flicked back on each stride to hit the gluteals. To improve posture during this activity, both hands can be held with their backs resting on the lower back, so that the heels touch them as they are lifted. In this way the athlete becomes more aware of the activity and can easily tell if the feet have not been picked up sufficiently.

Fast foot-toe running – 10m

This exercise is used to coordinate the arms and legs at speed. The athlete starts off by leaning forward slightly with the eyes looking down and forward. He or she then takes very short strides on the toes, at the same time moving the hands in synchronization with the feet. The movements must be performed as quickly as possible and there should be only very slow progress forward.

Long-stride (bounding) running – 30m

An excellent drill for conditioning the whole legs and mid-region core muscles. The athlete runs, but with long strides to 'hang' the leading knee at hip height for as long as possible in each stride. The movement should look like the middle stepping phase in the triple jump, and the athlete should be trying to gain height on each stride to ensure that enough time is spent in the air to hold the body in position. If the strides are too short, the exercise is pointless.

Foot-flick-back running.   *Fast foot-toe running.*   *Long-stride (bounding) running.*

Foot-snap running – 30m

An athlete must have good conditioning before attempting this drill. He or she runs steadily forward, lifting the lead leg so that it is level with the hips and then snapping the foot to the ground, landing it flat on the ball of the foot while maintaining good upright posture. The landing of the foot should be a slap rather than a stamp, indicating that it is moving backwards rather than landing dead.

Driving starts – 30m

These drills mimic the start of the sprint, in which the athlete needs to drive powerfully from the start line, head down and leaning forward.

This establishes a strong acceleration and uses the pushing muscles of the upper leg rather than the pulling muscles of the hamstrings and gluteals. The exercise should be performed to exaggerate the head-down forward-leaning aspects of the running movement and should not be continued beyond the distance that the athlete can manage. Although the endurance runner rarely uses such powerful accelerations, it is nevertheless a useful activity for developing a balanced approach to running.

Hill running – 20–40m

This activity is often ignored when it comes to posture, but by running up hills the athlete learns to lift the knees and run with excellent

LEFT: *Foot-snap running.*

ABOVE: *Driving starts.*

Step running.

Low hurdling.

technique. An incline of 20–40 degrees should be used, the angle increasing as the athlete learns to cope with the effort required to run fast up such slopes. The strides can either be short or long, the latter being much more difficult to achieve and requiring better power and suppleness. The activity should always be performed as quickly as possible.

Step running

This is an excellent means of establishing a clear, regular rhythm in runners. Because the steps are always the same distance apart, the skill needed to perform fast step running involves a set rhythmical pattern. The arms should always be coordinated with the feet, as in fast foot-toe running (*see* page 63). One, two, three or four steps at a time can be used, each requiring an increase in power. Youngsters should always start with one step at a time – as they grow more proficient, greater numbers of step separations can then be used. Flights of forty to eighty steps should be used initially, and can be increased each week as the athlete improves.

Low hurdle drills

Hurdle drills are often ignored by endurance runners but are again an excellent way of inculcating rhythm and power into the strides. Since the purpose is to establish rhythm, not train for hurdling, only very low hurdles should used and in series of quite large numbers (start with ten in a sequence, increasing the number each week as the athlete improves). In addition, the athlete must use both legs as the lead to ensure balanced development.

FOCUSED POSTURAL RUNNING

The above activities condition the body so that it can perform the running action correctly. However, for the endurance athlete time is limited for such activities, so it is during the actual running process that much of the work must be carried out. It is certainly better to perform technical running on a good, flat surface – preferably a track – since any undulations or slopes will change the action. It is simple enough for the coach to watch the athlete perform a lap of the track or indeed shorter repetitions, and then to make comments on what he or she sees.

In common with participants of more technical events, it is vital that the endurance athlete receives understandable feedback and that errors and problems are resolved by a firm non-acceptance of mistakes. In technical sessions, the time for the repetitions should be predetermined within a fairly comfortable range, so that rather than speed being of the essence, the athlete can concentrate on the running action instead. The coach in this situation is able to create the correct learning environment in which the discourse between athlete and coach is not strained and explanations can be put into effect in a non-stressful way.

It is also useful for the athlete to view good examples of running action and then to compare these with his or her own. Great understanding can come from observation of real examples, and some athletes will understand better what is being said by the coach if it is combined with such visual feedback. Inevitably,

some very famous runners have had bad technique, but this must be accepted as part of the overall appraisal of the variation between athletes rather than as the correct way to perform. Indeed, if such runners had improved their technique, they could, perhaps, have done even better!

POINTS OF OBSERVATION

Very often the coach will observe the athlete from the side. This is, of course, very instructional. However, it is also worth looking from both the front and the back in order to spot any errors that might be visible only from these viewpoints. It may come as a surprise to see how unbalanced some runners are when viewed from the rear, and indeed this is an excellent position to look for any rotation or lateral imbalance the runner may have. Video can be used to enhance the coach's observations, and again this feedback can be demonstrated to the athlete so that he or she can understand the problems more clearly.

SUMMARY

- Every athlete must strive to attain the best technique possible in order to maximize the efficiency of energy usage. This is a learnt process that can be greatly enhanced with a range of drills and exercises specifically designed to improve technical faults.
- While corrections to running technique come about only slowly and with great perseverance, the results can be extraordinarily effective in improving times in the endurance events. Just a tiny improvement in each stride can mean a significant improvement to the end result, as it will be repeated many thousands of times in each race.

CHAPTER 5

Mobility, Range of Movement and Suppleness

Mobility and suppleness are often confused. Mobility is the physical range that is allowed by a joint, while suppleness is the range allowed by the soft tissues regardless of the joint mobility. Thus, an athlete can be potentially very mobile but not very supple because his or her muscles, tendons and ligaments restrict movement.

The role of the coach in all this is to ensure that the athlete has as much suppleness as is needed to perform the required movements of his or her sport in the most effective manner. Restrictions to suppleness can cause a deterioration in running technique and reduced injury tolerance, thereby leading to a drop-off in performance. Some athletes take suppling further than is required, which can be equally counterproductive because it deadens the responses of the muscles that ordinarily assist in the event. Suppling should be performed as an everyday part of the training routine, but not to excess. It can be varied and made interesting, and it can also be used as part of a session or on its own.

SUPPLING

You often see runners stretching vigorously immediately prior to a race or fast run. This is the first no-no of suppling. If performed correctly, suppling is exhausting and works the muscles, tendons and ligaments to a stage where the athlete could not possibly perform maximally after having completed a session. This is because the muscles are stretched to their limits, thus inducing micro-tears that, if not allowed to repair, can develop into a full-blown injury. In addition, the neuromuscular responses to stretching (the stretch reflex mechanisms) become exhausted after a vigorous session and normal function does not return for several minutes or more.

HOW MUCH IS REQUIRED?

There are two schools of thought on just how much suppling athletes should do. The first suggests that everyone overstretches and that only the range needed for the event is required. The second is that the athlete should be well balanced and supple beyond what is required for the event in order to reduce the risk of injury when the inevitable incorrect movement is made.

There are arguments for both sides. The former ensures that overstretching cannot occur and that the muscles are always at their best responsive level. However, should the athlete make a technical error, the range of movement may well be too little to prevent a serious muscle pull. Increased suppling, on the other hand, may well reduce the muscular responsiveness a little, but it does guarantee that the athlete can cope with the odd error in technique without ripping the muscles to bits. Of the two, the majority of coaches tend to prefer the second option, but excellent results have been obtained using both approaches. The key is to make sure that the athlete's technique does not suffer because he or she is too unsupple to perform the correct movements with ease.

WARMING UP

The warm-up before a race should include loosening, not suppling, which is defined as movements of 90–95 per cent maximum range for the chosen action. Any more will simply reduce performance and possibly induce injury. Warm-up exercises should involve all the muscles of the body and should be performed in a reasonably dynamic yet relaxed way to enhance neuromuscular coordination. Thus, sitting on the ground stretching is not what is needed. The exercises should be performed as part of detailed structure involving a gradually progressive focus towards the competition.

RANGE OF MOVEMENT

In this chapter a range of exercises to help runners improve suppleness is described. These exercises are just a selection of those available but nevertheless are effective and useful in helping the athlete achieve the best results. The athlete should be tested for range of movement before the exercises are selected, as it is vital that the body is balanced up first (for more on this, *see* Chapter 9). Specific exercises must then be performed to correct any errors; only when this has been done should sessions be developed to cover the whole body.

In all forms of exercise, movement is produced by the muscles applying force and using the bones as levers, the joints being the pivot points, or fulcra. Each joint, be it elbow or knee, has a finite or maximum range of movement for the individual concerned, some lesser and some greater. This maximal range of movement is called the 'full mobility' of that joint. Normal active range approaches the full range only when there are no restrictions to movement, such as large muscles or injuries. It is therefore vital that athletes retain or even extend their normal range of movement to as close to full mobility as is required for their specific event.

A lack of suppleness is often associated with muscle weakness, as the muscles cannot be strengthened over their full range. The inevitable consequences of this are incorrect posture and stability, as well as the inability of the athlete to maintain the correct body position during exercise.

As athletes train, they invariably increase muscle tone and bulk, even if their overall size does not seem to change, although this is less significant in endurance athletes. Paradoxically, such improvements to the muscles create resistance to movement. Young athletes in particular tend to become very unsupple as a result of their training. The joints themselves are not restrictive, but the increased muscle tone and size cause a reduced suppleness. Unless this is corrected, it will cause a degradation in the range of applying force and therefore reduced performance. Problem areas that are most often noticed are the hamstrings of runners, who work very hard on these muscles yet still manage to injure them. In many instances the reason is that the hip flexors become tight and thus force the hamstrings to work too hard as they pull the leg back in the running action.

Mobility and suppleness are therefore related but are not the same, and the coach must be able to ascertain where any problems lie. An illustration of this, testing the Achilles tendon, shows how it can be done.

In the test the athlete squats as low as possible, with the head up and back straight. An acceptable degree of suppleness of the Achilles tendon will allow the athlete to reach a position with the top of the thighs parallel with the ground and the feet firmly flat. If there is restricted range of ankle flexion, the heels will lift the athlete onto the toes as he or she squats down. The problem can, however, have two main causes, one being a lack of suppleness of the calf/Achilles tendon and the other being insufficient mobility in the ankle joints to allow the required flexion. The former can be corrected but the latter cannot.

Understanding that some runners simply cannot achieve the necessary range of movement for their event is equally as important as realizing that some simply do not work hard enough to achieve that range. Whichever is the problem, the coach must be aware of it; if he or she is not, the athlete should seek professional advice.

METHODS OF SUPPLING

There are basically three methods of stretching, each requiring care and precision:

1. The passive method. Here, the movement is performed slowly and is held at the final point for a number of seconds before relaxing. Such slow movements prevent the stretch reflexes from activating and causing sudden contractions that may potentially result in injury. This is the most commonly used suppling method – and the simplest.
2. The dynamic approach, which is often spurned as being potentially injurious, and indeed can be if performed without care. This method involves moving into positions of stretch dynamically, so that the momentum of the movement overcomes any stretch reflex and extends the tendon/muscle unit accordingly. If the stretch is performed too fast, the unit can be damaged, but if it is performed with care it produces very effective results.
3. Proprioceptive neuromuscular facilitation (PNF) stretching, which involves the reduction of the stretch reflex (and thus the natural resistance to muscle lengthening) by contracting the muscle statically prior to stretching. This has proved to be very effective and is best actioned with two athletes working together, one to resist the contraction and apply the stretch and the other being stretched. The contraction should last around six seconds, followed by the stretch and hold for another six seconds, all repeated six times

BASIC SUPPLING ROUTINE

Ideally, athletes should supple for at least twenty minutes per day and should use a logical approach to the order of the session. A simple procedure is the most effective, starting with the neck and working systematically down the body. Most stretching exercises, including those listed below, are best performed five or six times each, with a six-second hold at the final position where applicable, followed by a ten- to fifteen-second rest between stretches. This will create effective adaptation within the tendon/muscle unit without causing damage.

Neck stretch

It is very important not to overstretch the neck, as the vertebrae here are small and are easily damaged by overvigorous flexion. In particular,

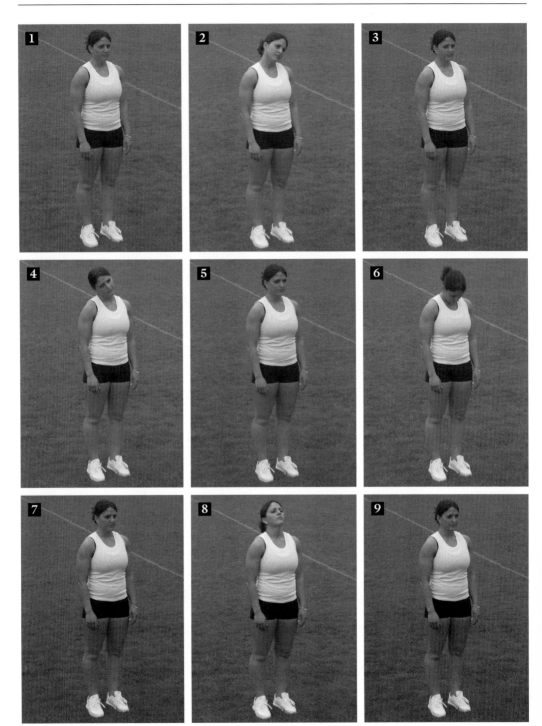

extreme backwards movements of the head should be avoided as these tend to compress the vertebral spines, with obvious deleterious effects. In addition, sideways stretches should be applied carefully, although they tend to be less potentially damaging. The forward range is safe and is very useful in stretching not only the muscles of the neck but also the nerves emanating from them.

Neck stretches should be performed slowly and carefully, and should never go beyond the range of pain. Athletes often have 'cricked' necks after cramping during sleep; these should always be treated with great care and never eased by forced movement. Massage is far more effective than stretching in easing such symptoms and returning neck mobility to normal.

Isolated shoulder rotations

This movement is performed by slowly rotating the shoulders both forwards and backwards, using the trapezius, upper back and pectoral muscles to produce an exaggerated rotation.

OPPOSITE PAGE:
Neck stretch.

THIS PAGE:
Isolated shoulder rotations.

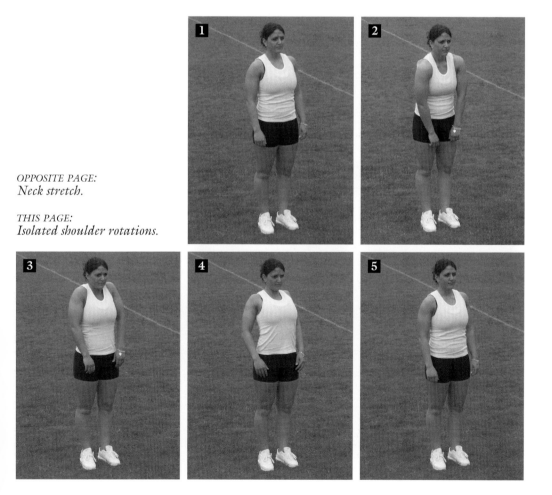

THIS PAGE:
Shoulder and arm rotations.

OPPOSITE PAGE:
Forward and backward shoulder stretches.

Shoulder and arm rotations

The classic shoulder and arm suppling exercise is performed best with both arms while holding a Cliniband, rope or stick to maintain a constant distance between them. A non-elastic imple-ment is better for the purpose because it can then be used to measure progress.

Forward and backward shoulder stretches

This movement is achieved by moving the arms both forwards across the body at shoulder level using the pectorals, and then backwards behind the shoulders at the same level by activating the rhomboid and posterior deltoid muscles. The movement should be performed slowly and precisely, and should be held at the extreme ends of the ranges for about six seconds.

Standing side stretch

Often the sideways movement of the body is completed ineffectively, leading to a lack of suppleness in the involved muscles. It is best performed by leaning to one side and simul-taneously extending the opposite arm above the head and reaching it over towards the bending side. This produces a very effective stretch along the full range of each side.

THIS PAGE:
Standing side stretch.

OPPOSITE PAGE:
Standing mid-region rotation.

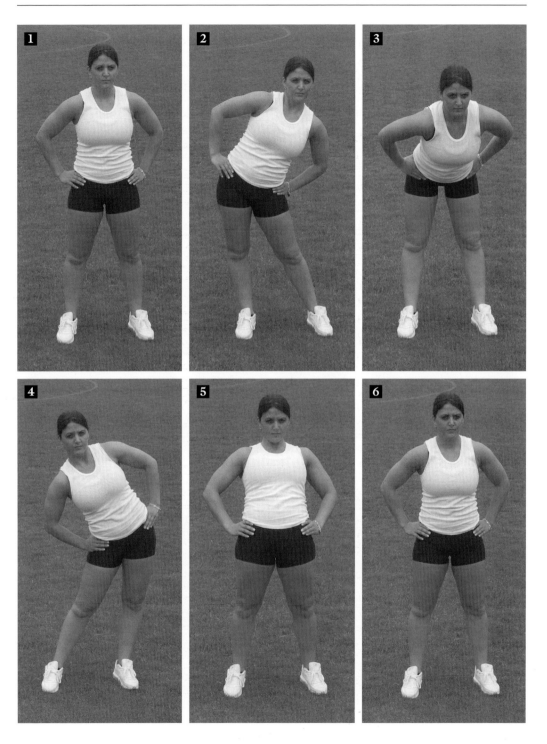

Standing mid-region rotation

This is a general exercise that can also be used to stretch the particular muscles involved. It is performed by standing with the feet wide apart to fix the hips, and then rotating the shoulders slowly round to one side as far as possible. This position is held for about six seconds, after which the shoulders are rotated to the other side and the position is held again. Care should be taken to keep the movement steady and evenly balanced, although there may be some difference in range from side to side.

Spinal-curve stretch – forwards flexion

It is important to keep the full length of the spine supple, something that can be achieved through spinal curve stretches. The flexing version requires the athlete to lie on his or her back and take the legs over the head so that the feet are as close to the ground as possible. Curvature can be increased by bending the knees and trying to touch them rather than the toes on the ground. The final position should be held for about six seconds. Some lateral stretch can be applied by walking the toes to either side.

OPPOSITE PAGE:
Spinal-curve stretch –
forwards flexion.

THIS PAGE:
Spinal-curve stretch –
backwards extension
(standing).

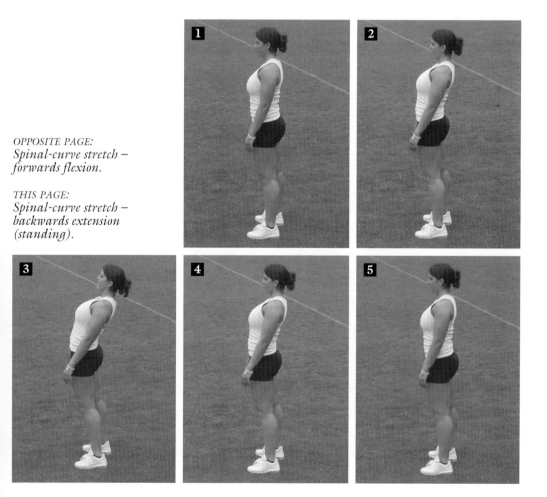

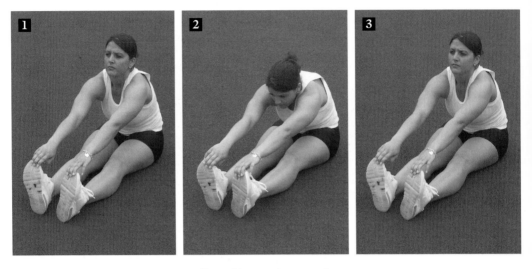

Seated hamstring stretch.

Spinal-curve stretch – backwards extension

If this movement is performed standing, great care must be taken as too much hyperextension of the back can impact on the vertebral spines. The safest method is to lie backward over a large inflatable ball so that the stretch can be released simply by rolling sideways. The object of the stretch is to relax the muscles of the back and stretch over the ball with the arms and legs extended. As with most of the other stretching exercises, this position should be held for about six seconds.

Seated hamstring stretch

This is the easiest controllable hamstring stretch exercise. It is performed sitting on the ground or half on a bench (about the height of one used for physiotherapy) with one leg resting on the ground and supporting the body, and the other leg (the one being stretched) extended along the edge of the bench. The arms are extended horizontally to prevent back rounding and the head is held up facing forward. The abdomen is then pushed forward towards the feet and the toes are pulled back towards the body as the stretch is progressed. The stretched position is held for about six seconds and then the exercise is repeated on the other leg.

Hurdle-position hamstring stretch

This is a classic exercise in which the athlete sits on the ground in a similar position to that assumed during hurdling (front leg straight out in front, rear leg held behind at ninety degrees with the knee also bent at that angle). The back is held straight and then the hands are pushed forward to the toes; this end position is held for three to four seconds. This is repeated, working on extra range each time without sacrificing the straight back position. Note that the front leg must also be held straight to ensure maximum effectiveness. Once one leg has been stretched, the alternate leg position is adopted and the movement is repeated. It is essential that good position is adopted for this exercise, so some initial stretching work may be needed before it is attempted.

Hurdle-position hamstring stretch.   *Standing hamstring stretch.*

Lying hip-flexor stretch.

Standing hamstring stretch

This is a commonly used exercise for improving hamstring suppleness but is less controllable and less effective than the seated version above. The exercise is performed by standing and resting the leg being stretched on a hurdle or wall that is at a comfortable height. The body is then pressed toward the thigh as in the seated version of the exercise, so that the hamstrings and gluteals are stretched. Care must be taken not to curve the back over as this gives a false impression of the actual suppleness. The final position is held for about six seconds and the stretch is then repeated on the other side.

Lying hip-flexor stretch

One the most important advances in the understanding of athletic performance has come with the realization that the hip flexors are not only a very important part of leg movement but also of basic core stability. It has since become clear that many back problems originate with a lack of suppleness in this area.

One of the most effective exercises to improve suppleness of the hip flexors is best performed with two people. The person to be stretched lies on a physiotherapy bench or similar with one buttock on and one off, and the body lying along the bench. The leg being stretched is then lowered and extended towards the ground, while the lower back is held flat on the bench and the non-active leg is held bent up at ninety degrees. The helper controls and stabilizes the movement. Gravity provides the stretching force, but in cases of great weakness the weight of the leg may be partially taken by the helper.

Split-leg hip-flexor stretch

This exercise is also very effective in stretching the hip flexors and can be carried out without

Spilt-leg hip-flexor stretch.

81

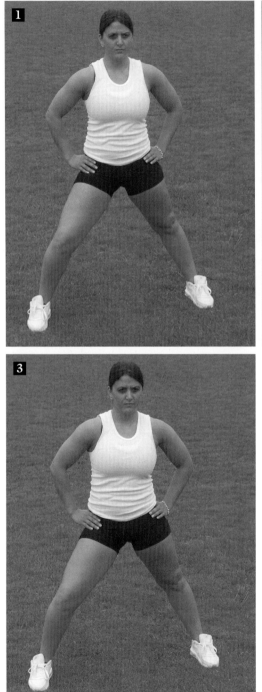

THIS PAGE:
Standing adductor stretch.

OPPOSITE PAGE:
Standing abductor stretch.

the aid of a bench. It is performed by kneeling on one knee, pushing the other foot well forward into a wide split position, and placing the hands behind the back. From here, the hips are pushed forward while the shoulders are held back. The final position is held for six seconds before relaxation and then repetition on the other side. It is very important that the hips are in a forward position; if they are not, the lower back will take the strain.

Standing adductor stretch

The adductors can be stretched simply by placing the legs well astride and pushing the hips to one side, and holding the position for six seconds. Alternatively, bend forward towards the ground. When the maximum sideways split is achieved, the athlete then gently stands up, thus applying the stretch. This exercise must be performed carefully and slowly, and the final position should be held for the usual six seconds.

Standing abductor stretch

This is performed by crossing over the leg that is being stretched in front of the other. The body is then carefully and slowly bent to the same side as the foot of the stretch leg, thus forming a curve with the body and stretching the abductors.

Standing quadriceps stretch

Suppleness in the quadriceps is most important for all athletic events but is often neglected. This stretch is performed by standing on

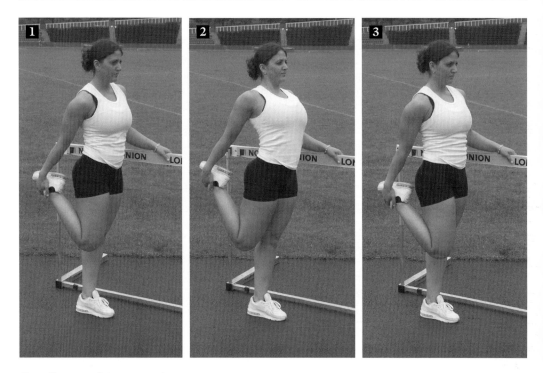

Standing quadriceps stretch.

one leg, grasping the ankle of the leg that is being stretched from the rear and pulling it up and away from the buttocks. The final position is held for six seconds and the leg is then relaxed before the exercise is repeated on the other side. Because of the large muscle bulk of the quadriceps, considerable work is required for progress to be made and up to ten stretches can be performed without deleterious effect.

Seated calf stretch

The calf/Achilles tendon units are very susceptible to injury, so it is vital that they have maximum suppleness, especially as the feet are the primary contact points – and therefore force application points – with the ground in all events. A number of effective exercises can be used to improve suppleness in this area, one of the most controllable and effective of these being the seated stretch. In this the athlete sits on the ground with legs straight out and together. The balls of the feet are grasped firmly and pulled steadily towards the body, the final position being held for the usual six seconds. The toes are then pointed and pulled back again. It is important that the calves remain relaxed during the movement to avoid invoking the stretch reflex.

Standing calf stretch

The calves can also be stretched in a controlled manner by standing with one foot back to the point where the heel is about 10cm off the ground, with body leaning forward

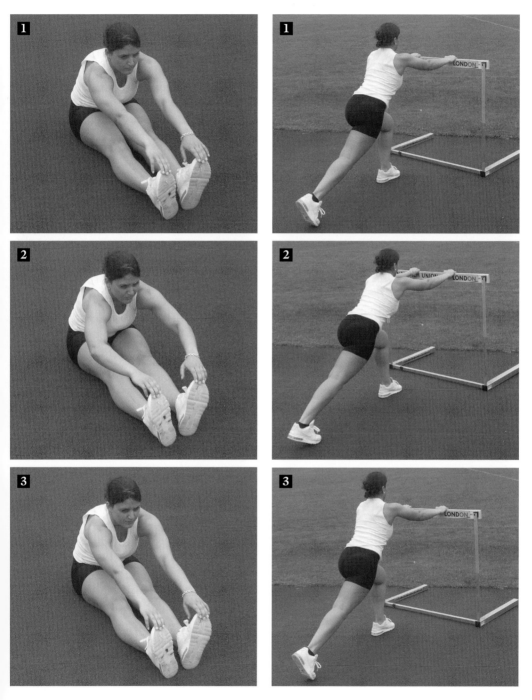

Seated calf stretch.

Standing calf stretch.

and supported. The body is then pushed back steadily and, at the same time, the stretched calf is relaxed. After holding the final position for six seconds, the pressure is released for about ten seconds and the movement is repeated. If the heel is able to touch the ground, the foot should be moved further back for the next repetition.

EVENT SPECIFICS

Running in general requires little beyond the basic suppling, but more specialized events like hurdling and steeplechasing need a greater range of movement in the hips, lower back and associated muscles. Walking is a little different again, in that the range of movement of the ankles (calf/Achilles units) must be maximized, and thus suppleness in those areas is paramount. In all running and walking events, athletes tend to focus on the lower body, but it is essential that every region of the body is suppled properly to ensure that maximum force can be applied efficiently through a relaxed full range, and that correct posture can be maintained during both training and competition.

SUMMARY

- Confusion over the understanding of the terms suppleness and mobility has often led athletes to work in the wrong way to improve their range of movement.
- Coaches must fully understand the difference between suppleness and mobility, and they must also be able to analyse an athlete's needs in the correct way. If this is not done, injuries and loss of performance may result. This also applies to the difference between loosening and suppling, since the former will be sufficient for preparation before a race while the latter is a means of improving the range of movement but should not be performed close to a race or hard running session.
- Although improvements in suppleness come only from consistent sheer hard work, they are sometimes miraculous in terms of improved performance and a reduction in injuries.
- All runners must work on their suppleness. A failure to do so will lead to increasing problems and a significant reduction in progress.

CHAPTER 6

Core Stability Conditioning

During running, the legs propel the body forward and the upper body largely acts simply to balance the rotating movements of the hips during each stride. This means that the mid-region – the area of the body connecting the legs to the upper body – is in continual use during running, not only supporting the upper body but also stabilizing the posture. This mid-region of the body is called the 'core', which is where the term 'core stability' comes from.

The core involves all the muscles that protect and stabilize the abdomen, hips, pelvis and lower back. The most outwardly visible of these is the rectus abdominis muscle, popularly known as the six-pack, which is very evident in well-trained runners. This muscle is shown in Fig. 7 in relation to the other external muscles of the anterior abdomen and thorax. The diagram shows clearly just how important this muscle is in maintaining posture, and yet it is only one of many that keep the core in balance.

Many of the core muscles are internal. For example, the oblique and transversus muscles lie around the sides of the abdomen and are attached to the pelvis, spine and ribs. They are flat, strong muscles that control lateral and rotational movement, and they form the compartment of the abdominal cavity. The hip-flexor muscles (psoas and ilio-psoas), meanwhile, run from the internal spine and out under the abdominal muscles to the top of the femur.

Lifting the knee therefore applies force right through the body core to the spine. If the hip-flexor muscles are weak or short, it can be seen

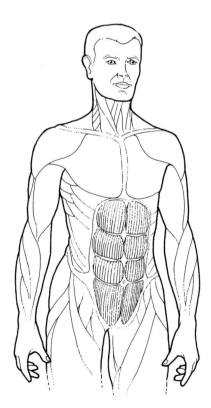

Fig. 7 Rectus abdominis muscles of the body core.

87

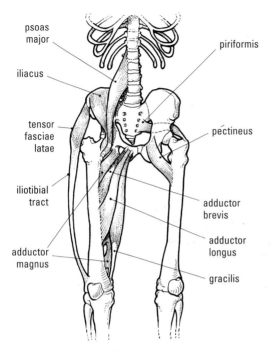

Fig. 8 Internal abdominal core stability muscles.

Labels on figure:
- psoas major
- iliacus
- tensor fasciae latae
- iliotibial tract
- adductor magnus
- piriformis
- pectineus
- adductor brevis
- adductor longus
- gracilis

that the mere action of running will produce large stresses in the lower back. This connection is not always appreciated by runners or their coaches, and if ignored can lead to career-ending back problems.

The structure of the internal muscles that control the relationship between the body core and the active leg is shown clearly in Fig. 8. From this it can be seen just how complex the core and its structural components are, and also how important they are in allowing an individual to run in a balanced fashion without injury. It is for this reason that core stability is now recognized as a key component in the training of all athletes and essential to the improvement of performance and avoidance of injury.

It is now accepted that core stability training should be a separate and specific session rather than simply a small part of regular gym work. This actually makes it easier for the coach and athlete to look out for areas of weakness and to perform proper conditioning to correct these problems.

The drudgery of performing mid-region exercises has also largely been replaced by the use of Swiss and medicine balls. As a result, a huge range of exercises can now be utilized that allow much more interesting yet still effective ways of working the required muscles. The exercises described in the remainder of this chapter are just a small selection of those that can be used. They have been chosen to give examples of the different types of exercise rather an exhaustive list of all possibilities.

CORE STABILITY MUSCLE STRENGTHENING

This type of strengthening differs from that used to strengthen the muscles that move the limbs. The reason for this is that in order to produce stability the core muscles operate in a near-isometric way – that is, they contract but do not produce movement, a little like the guy ropes that support a tent. In addition, the muscles contract over a much greater time period. A simple example of this is a guardsman standing to attention for several hours. The product of such apparent lack of activity is intense fatigue, particularly in the lower back. It is only through the constant practice of standing still that the fatigue diminishes and the soldier is able to remain comfortably on guard, indicating that he has developed very strong core stabilizing muscles and considerable endurance ability in these areas.

Athletes not only need to stand but also have to perform intense physical movements without letting their body's core section move out of place. They therefore need to perform exercises that will strengthen their core muscles, which by necessity should incorporate sufficiently lengthy contractions to ensure that the muscles can operate over the required timespan of the event. In modern-day competition this does not just mean the time it takes to perform the event, but also the time taken warming up and waiting to compete. A marathon runner needs to be able to maintain a good postural position for more than two hours during the race and also for a short time before setting off. A long-jumper or discus-thrower performs for much less time in active mode, but their competition can last as long as a marathon, and tiredness must not set in during that period. Athletes competing in these events must all therefore train their muscles in a similar manner to ensure that fatigue will not degrade their performance up to and including the duration of the competition.

There are a number of ways that the desired effect can be produced. These include bodyweight, weight and other resistance exercises, and medicine ball and Swiss ball conditioning. To benefit core stability, each of these activities must be performed in a similar manner to ensure that the positions attempted can be maintained for increasing lengths of time. This is the difference between core stability work and most other forms of conditioning.

ISOMETRIC MUSCLE CONTRACTION

When a muscle is contracted in a static position it is called an isometric contraction. Historically, such contractions have been used as a means of increasing muscle size and strength – in the 1950s, for example, bodybuilder Charles Atlas promoted the use of isometric exercises commercially for improving the physique. Since then, however, further work has shown that isometrics strengthen the muscles only over a very narrow range on either side of the static position adopted. This range extends to about fifteen degrees on either side, indicating that such exercise would be of little use in strengthening muscles used to produce movement. It does, however, suggest that isometric contractions could be very important in strengthening core stability muscles in a way similar to that in which they operate normally. This is, in fact, the case, since these muscles are more concerned with holding fixed postural positions rather than creating movement. This then defines the way in which core stability activities must be performed.

Taking the simple press-up as an example, the exercise requires the athlete to hold the body in a horizontal position supported by

Press-up position.

the arms and feet. The arms are bent so that the body is lowered to the ground, and are then extended to raise it to the initial position. This seems simple enough, but consider what the core mid-region muscles must do when the body is lowered and then raised. They must fix the whole body in a straight line over a period of up to a minute if a set of twenty press-ups is performed. Since no movement of the mid-region is required, the core stability muscles are acting isometrically for the whole of this time. Athletes with poor core stability will have difficulty doing this and will wobble and sag during the movements. This is a clear indication that more conditioning is needed in the mid-region area, something that can be achieved through isometric strength endurance work.

BODY-WEIGHT EXERCISES

Core stability body-weight exercises are performed isometrically and include any that use only the athlete's body weight. Because this form of training can be boring, the coach should use his or her imagination to invent and apply a range of activities. Different sessions used in rotation over a period of weeks can make it more bearable and so will help to keep the athlete on focus.

Each exercise is performed for a defined period of time followed by a period of rest. Initially, this should be a hold of twenty seconds and a recovery of thirty seconds. This is repeated four times for each exercise. Each week, the hold time is increased by ten seconds up to a maximum of ninety seconds, after which a new exercise with a similar effect should be introduced. The recovery time should be kept at thirty seconds. Where the exercise uses one leg or arm at a time, four sets are performed on each side to ensure development is balanced.

OPPOSITE PAGE:
Press-up position with reverse leg raise.

The other important factor is to ensure that correct posture is used in all exercises. This means that sufficient suppleness of the soft tissue and mobility of the joints must be a precursor to working on core stability. If an athlete is too stiff to achieve good neutral positions, there is no way that he or she should attempt the more difficult core stability exercises.

Examples of body-weight exercises which strengthen core stability are given below, although this list is by no means comprehensive:

Press-up position

This is performed by adopting the initial press-up position as seen on page 89.

Press-up position with reverse leg raise

The press-up starting position is adopted, then one leg is raised above horizontal to the rear and held there.

Press-up position with leg and arm raise

The press-up starting position is taken up, but in this case one arm and the opposite leg are raised and held in position.

Standing knee raise

The athlete stands on one leg, arms held out horizontally in front, with one knee raised so that the top of the thigh is parallel with the ground. This must be performed with the hips held in the same position as for standing on two legs, and the athlete must ensure that the lower back is not allowed to curve outwards as the knee is raised.

Standing outward-rotated knee raise

This is performed as for the standing knee raise except that the knee is rotated outwards to as near ninety degrees to the natural position as possible.

Standing inward-rotated knee raise

This is performed as for the standing knee raise, except that the knee is rotated inward and up towards the stomach.

Standing inclined leg raise

The athlete stands on one leg, hands held out horizontally in front, and carefully leans back about thirty degrees. At the same time, he or she raises one leg straight out to the front at the same angle, keeping the body and raised leg in a line. Note that this exercise should not be performed by athletes with lower back problems.

Lying hip raise

This is performed by lying on the ground with the hands by the sides. From here, the hips are raised off the ground. This is easier to perform if the legs are very slightly bent and the weight is taken on the heels and shoulders. The head and neck should remain relaxed to avoid strain.

Lying abductor raise

The athlete lies on his or her side with the body and legs in a straight line. The head is rested on the lower arm while the upper arm is bent and the hand rested on the ground for stability. From here, the upper leg is raised to about forty-five degrees (or higher if possible), keeping it in line with the body. There should be no rotation of the hip and the foot should remain parallel to the ground.

Standing outward-rotated knee raise.

Standing inward-rotated knee raise.

THIS PAGE:
Standing inclined leg raise.

OPPOSITE PAGE:
Lying hip raise.

Lying abductor raise.

WEIGHT AND OTHER RESISTANCE EXERCISES

The addition of weights and other forms of resistance increases the difficulty in performing exercises, but their best use is in activities where the body is held in a fixed position and the weight or resistance is moved around this position. The exercises are not, therefore, performed as in the other core stability work, since a static position cannot be maintained while the weight is being retrieved and the initial position regained. And because the resistance applies considerable stress and the positions are difficult to hold for lengthy periods, these exercises are performed as sets of a small number of repetitions (for example, six sets of three)

BASIC WEIGHT TRAINING

Basic weight training has a high core stability conditioning element. For example, the simple back squat requires the athlete to fix the body position while the legs are flexed and then straightened. Since the weight is on the shoulders, considerable strain is created along the full length of the back, but because the effort seems to be in working the legs, the effect on the core is often ignored. However, any athlete who performs squats for the first time or after a lay-off knows only too well which muscles are being worked.

When performed properly, all weight exercises require considerable core stability. A properly balanced weights programme, in which the exercises are carried out with good technique and posture, will therefore give an athlete most of the core strength he or she needs. This is not to say that other core work is wasted, as there are always areas of weakness that weight training will not specifically help. It is to address these weaknesses that other work is needed, most often specific event stability

training. General weight training is explained in more detail in the companion title to this book, *Strength Training for Athletes*, also published by Crowood.

SWISS BALL EXERCISES

The Swiss ball is the most recent piece of equipment to be incorporated into training programmes, although it has been used for many years in such diverse activities as Pilates, remedial therapy and other related forms of exercise. It provides the athlete with an enjoyable yet hard form of training that can be adapted to use in both general and specific core stability work.

Strict back squat body position, in mid-lift.

Seated single-leg raise.

As with the other core stability activities, there are a wide range of exercises that can be used with a Swiss ball, thus making sessions interesting as well as fruitful. Some basic exercises are given below; again these are only a sample of what can be developed into a programme to ensure athletes are strong enough in the mid-region to perform their chosen event.

Seated single-leg raise

The athlete sits firmly on the Swiss ball with the body vertical, the arms outstretched, the thighs at ninety degrees to the body and the lower legs vertical. From here, the athlete moves slowly forwards until he or she is nearly falling off the ball, and the feet are adjusted so that they are again at a ninety-degree bend. One leg is then raised to the horizontal and held in position for the required time. It is then returned to the starting position and the other leg is raised.

Lying single-leg raise

In this exercise, the shoulders are rested on the ball with the body outstretched, arms held away from the body and the lower legs at ninety degrees. It is important that the body is held very firm and in line with the upper legs. From here, one leg is straightened to the horizontal and held in position. When the requisite time has elapsed, the starting position is regained and the other leg is lifted.

Lying sideways move

The starting position is the same as for the lying single-leg raise. From here, the shoulders are pushed to one side, with the upper body kept horizontal rather than twisted. Once the furthest position has been attained, it is held for the required time before repeating on the other side.

Single-arm raise with body in press-up position

For this exercise the feet are placed on the Swiss ball and a press-up position is adopted, with a firmly maintained straight body. From here, one arm is raised in line with the body and held in position; after the set time it is then returned to the ground and the exercise is repeated with the other arm.

Kneeling single-arm raise

This requires great skill. The athlete kneels on the ball with both hands also resting on it. When he or she is stable, one arm is raised to the horizontal. This is then repeated for the other arm. The difficulty lies in balancing, which is, of course, more difficult for weaker athletes.

Kneeling double-arm raise

Again, this requires great stability. The athlete kneels on the ball with the body vertical and arms down by the sides. From here, both arms are raised to the sides and held in position.

Kneeling single-arm single-leg raise

The starting position is the same as for the kneeling single-arm raise. From here, one arm and the opposite leg are raised to the horizontal and held there for the required time. The starting position is then regained and the opposite leg and arm are raised.

Feet-raised crunches

This is a simple yet effective exercise. The athlete lies on the ground face-up and places his or her feet on the ball with the legs at a ninety-degree bend. The shoulders and head are then lifted off the ground and that position is held for the set time.

OPPOSITE PAGE:
LEFT: *Lying single-leg raise.*
RIGHT: *Lying sideways move.*

THIS PAGE:
Single-arm raise with body in press-up position.

Kneeling single-arm raise.

Kneeling double-arm raise.

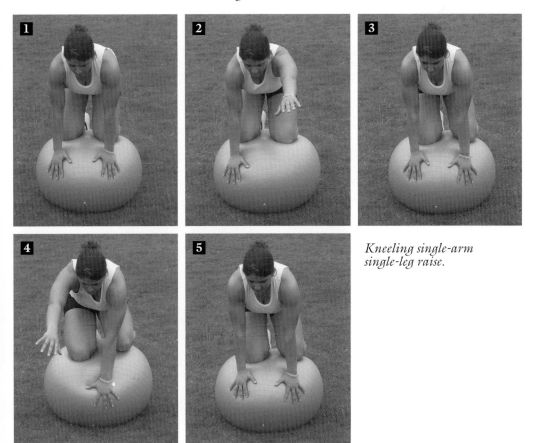

Kneeling single-arm single-leg raise.

Feet-raised crunches.

*Feet-raised arms-
outstretched crunches.*

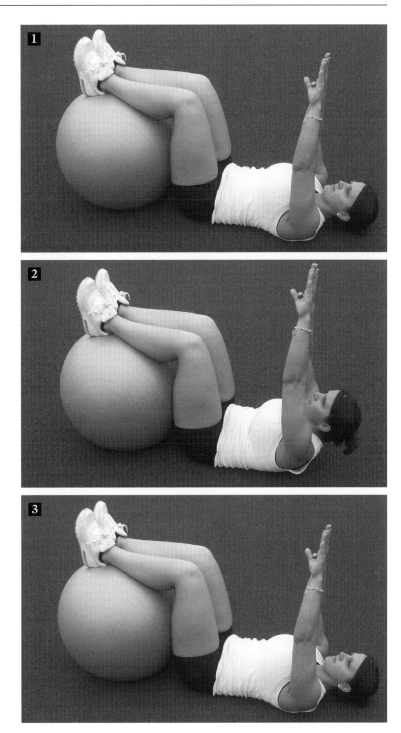

Feet-raised arms-outstretched crunches

This is similar to the feet-raised crunches except that the arms are held above the head for the duration of the exercise.

Variations on these exercises can be performed while standing on the Swiss ball, but this requires great skill and balance, and so should not be attempted by beginners or those with a fragile nature. It is wise to perform such exercises on a soft surface, as even the best athletes will occasionally fall off the ball.

Kneeling and standing on the Swiss ball can be a starting point for some very advanced and effective event-specific work, particularly for throwers. Such athletes can use these initial balancing positions to practise throwing movements with and without implements, but again beginners will not be able to perform this type of work easily. It takes great skill and perseverance to reach a stage where any movement at all can be performed while balancing on the ball.

In my view, Swiss balls are a major asset in the library of core endurance running stability conditioning techniques and can be used by all athletes at some level regardless of ability. They are inexpensive to purchase and simple to work with but, as always, it is only through practice that noticeable improvements will result.

MEDICINE BALL EXERCISES

The medicine ball is another handy tool for developing core stability. Because of its varied resistance it can be used for young and weak athletes as well as more experienced exponents. It is utilized mainly in a similar manner to the sand bag, as the athlete can move the medicine ball while maintaining fixed postural positions.

The main area of medicine ball use is in event-specific work, although many simple activities using this piece of equipment can be performed as a fun way of training the core without the boredom of simple static work. With imagination, a whole range of exercises can be developed and used in varied sessions, again giving the coach the luxury of applying interesting and enjoyable diversions to help relieve the grind of ordinary training. Group as well as individual work can also be used to help improve team spirit and harmony within the squad. (For more details *see Conditioning for Athletes*, published by Crowood.)

SUMMARY

- Core means centre or heart, so core stability is the centre or heart of stability and is the means by which our body holds its posture. If the muscles involved in this continuous process are weak or lack endurance, an athlete can only approximate the position he or she needs to maintain in order to perform well.
- Core stability conditioning can be achieved using a wide range of methods, all of which require hard work and perseverance. Because the activities can be widely varied, core stability training can be made fun and interesting. Only limited progress will be attained if the same activities are repeated endlessly.
- Once competence in core stability exercises has been achieved, athletes will find it much easier to perform the highly skilled movements required in their sport. Add to this the protection that a strong core gives, and the overall benefits of such conditioning are abundantly clear.

CHAPTER 7

Specific Circuit and Stage Training

Circuit training is, in a general sense, a universally excellent method of conditioning the body both aerobically and anaerobically. For the runner, however, it can have even more useful effects when modified slightly to strengthen weak areas, and specifically geared training sessions can be designed to suit the needs of the individual, both in full fitness and at times of injury. This chapter discusses the general principles of modifying circuits, as well as providing two specific examples, one for a runner who is weak in the back and shoulders and the other for a runner who is recovering from a hamstring pull.

MODIFYING CIRCUITS TO WORK ON WEAKNESSES

It is quite common to see runners who have an excellent leg action but who look very awkward when it comes to posture and arm action. Such runners will have paid little heed to their upper body, and so run with rounded shoulders and poor posture, and are unable to achieve maximum speed when called upon. In addition, their hips are often carried in a top-rotated-forward position that does not allow full knee lift. Circuit training is an excellent way to compensate for such problems in an aerobic yet specific way.

A basic schedule for a runner would follow the normal pattern of trying to include exercises that focus on every part of the body. However, when trying to improve upper-body weakness some of the exercises should be modified and extra ones slotted in to work those body areas that need attention, including the back, shoulders, neck and arms. So, as a starting point, a general session such as that given below should be introduced (note that the exercises listed in this chapter have, in the main, already been described in earlier chapters; only the newly introduced activities are described here):

Full squat jumps

See page 31.

Press-ups (half range)

See page 41.

Free flat sit-ups

See page 31.

Flat twisting-back hyperextensions

See page 31.

Chinnies

See page 26.

Squat jumps – full range, extending arms above head when jumping.

Squat thrusts

See page 26.

Supported narrow-stance alternate-leg split jumps

See page 131.

The next stage is to modify some of these exercises and to add two new ones that work on the arms, shoulders and back, so that the circuit is as below:

Full-range squat jumps

This is variation on the standard squat jump, in which the arms are thrown up above the head during the jump rather than being held behind it.

Press-ups (half/full range)

See page 41.

Free sit-ups, with arms extended

Performing the sit-up movement with the arms extended increases the range of movement and also aids its execution. However, care should be taken not to use the arms to provide momentum in order to make the exercise easier. Instead, try to carry them passively in the extended position rather than throwing them forward.

Flat hyperextensions, with arms extended

Performing back hyperextensions with the arms extended forward gives more prominence to the upper back during the exercise. It is a variation on the basic movement and is useful as a change of emphasis for the athlete.

Chinnies

See page 26.

Double-arm dumb-bell sprint arm action

This is a variation on the standard dumb-bell sprint action whereby both arms are moved over the range together rather than in opposite directions (alternate arms version). This produces excellent stretching, plus work on the deltoids, upper back and shoulders. Start off with 2.5kg dumb-bells.

Squat thrusts

See page 26.

Feet-raised bench dips

See page 31.

Supported narrow-stance alternate-leg split jumps

See page 131.

This modified session transforms the original circuit into one that will focus on exercising the arms, back and shoulders much more specifically, while still maintaining an overall aerobic effect.

Another example of a situation where specific circuits can be used to good effect is when an athlete has been laid up with a hamstring pull and has done little running for several weeks. Once the physiotherapist has reported that the injury has passed through its initial healing stage, it is vital that the athlete proceeds through a period of rehabilitation to strengthen and condition the damaged region before full training is resumed. A

THIS PAGE:
Free sit-ups, with arms extended.

OPPOSITE PAGE:
Flat hyperextensions, with arms extended.

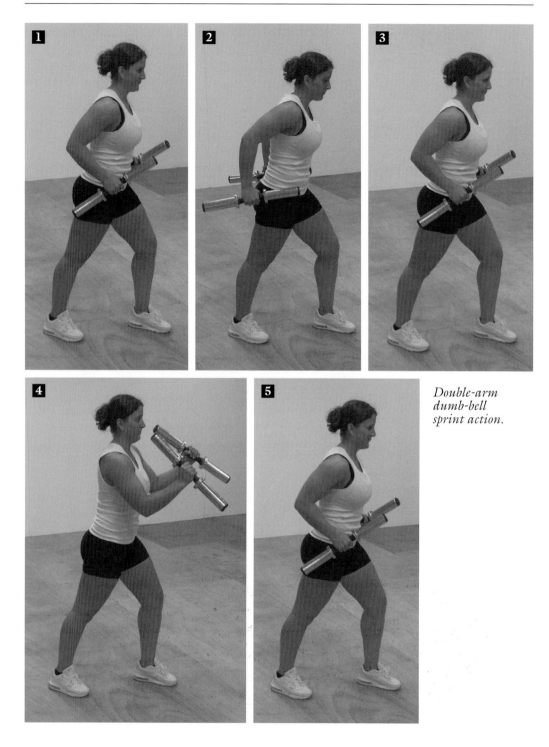

Double-arm dumb-bell sprint action.

modified specific circuit will help with this rehabilitation process, and will enable the athlete to move into a steadily increasing period of training without the stress of trying to run hard when this is physically inappropriate.

Starting again with the basic schedule for a runner given on pages 109–10, the circuit can be modified to suit the needs of the injured athlete. This time the resulting session can be used to continue recovery once the athlete is back in a training build-up, and from then on.

Full squat jumps

See page 31.

Press-ups (half range)

See page 41.

Alternate-leg reverse raises

See page 41.

Free sit-ups

See page 31.

Flat feet-held hyperextensions

This is another modified back hyperextension, in which the feet are held down so that the upper body alone lifts off the ground.

Alternate-leg 'V' sits

See page 31.

Squat thrusts

See page 26.

Step-in step-up drives

See page 47.

Supported narrow-stance alternate-leg split jumps

See page 131.

Bench step-up drives

See page 47.

This modified session will now work the hamstrings, gluteals and lower back harder than the general session and will certainly aid the process of reconditioning the damaged area.

THE PRINCIPLES OF MODIFYING CIRCUITS

The two sessions given above and their modifications are examples of how to change basic circuits to suit your aim. The principles of this are:

1. Ascertain what the athlete's weaknesses are and what areas of the body are involved.
2. Draw up a general circuit that would suit the athlete if he or she was uninjured or had no weaknesses.
3. Finally, modify the circuit by changing the emphasis of some of the exercises that are included, introducing new ones that work the specific areas required and replacing any that are inappropriate.

A more detailed analysis of the use of such sessions to aid recovery is included at the end of this chapter.

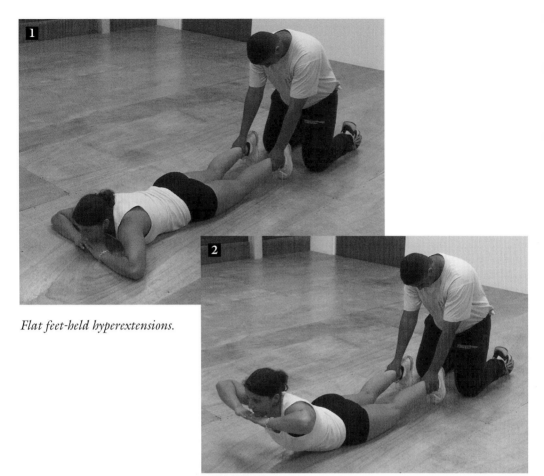

Flat feet-held hyperextensions.

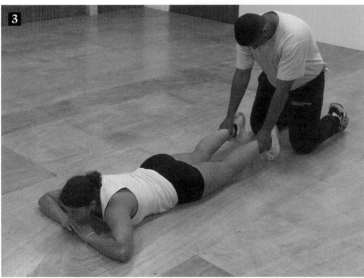

RUNNING-SPECIFIC BODY-WEIGHT STAGE TRAINING

A specific programme of body-weight stage training aimed at the runner is one of the best conditioning methods for introducing local muscular endurance and improving on weaknesses highlighted by the coach.

Session 1 below has been designed to work specifically on a weakness in the muscles of the lower back, while Session 2 and Session 3 improve general core stability in the mid-region and lower back.

Note that many of the exercises listed here have already been described in earlier chapters of this book; therefore only newly introduced activities are described below. Suggested initial repetitions are indicated after each exercise as follows: beginner; intermediate; advanced.

Session 1

Alternate leg step-in step up drives – 8/8; 10/10; 12/12

See page 47.

Kneeling alternate-arm/leg raises – 2/2

This is another good exercise for the core stability muscles. The hold time starts off at eight seconds, followed by an eight-second rest, and is increased by one second per week.

The athlete starts off on all fours with the thighs and arms vertical. From here, one arm and the opposite leg are raised and held for a set time at the horizontal, after which the starting position is resumed. The other arm and its opposite leg are then raised and held in position. Care must be taken not to sag or rock during the movements (the hold time can be reduced if the athlete is incapable of sustaining a good position). This exercise is repeated after every other exercise in the session.

Chinnies – 6/6; 9/9; 12/12

See page 26.

Kneeling alternate-arm/leg raises – 2/2

See above.

Double-leg reverse leg raises – 6; 9; 12

This exercise is excellent for strengthening the lower back, gluteals and hamstrings.

The athlete lies face-down and holds on to a solid bar or bench with the arms above the head. Without lifting the shoulders, both legs are kept straight and raised from the hips. The lifted position is then held for three seconds and the legs lowered back to the starting position.

Kneeling alternate-arm/leg raises – 2/2

See above.

Full squat jumps with ground touch – 6; 9; 12

This is a variation on the full squat jump in which the hands are used to gauge the depth of leg bend.

The starting position is in the crouch with the hands touching the ground. From here, the athlete jumps vertically and vigorously to full extension, returning to the starting point and then jumping again as the hands touch the ground. The set is thus continuous and performed smoothly.

Kneeling alternate-arm/leg raises – 2/2

See above.

Kneeling alternate-leg/arm reverse raises.

Double-leg reverse leg raises.

OPPOSITE PAGE:
Reverse body-bridge press-ups.

Reverse body-bridge press-ups – 6; 9; 12

This is a tricky exercise to perform in that it requires good range of movement in the shoulders. The athlete adopts a body-bridge position facing upwards, with the legs out straight and the arms supporting the shoulders vertically. The body must be held firm and horizontal, and there must be no sagging at the hips. Once the body is stable, the arms are flexed as deeply as possible and then extended.

Kneeling alternate-arm/leg raises – 2/2

See above.

Twisting crunches – 6/6; 9/9; 12/12

This is a variation on the feet-raised crunch exercise (*see* page 131) and introduces work on the oblique and transversus muscle groups. The athlete lies on the ground face-up and raises the legs (you can use a bench for support) so that the knee and hip angles are at ninety degrees. The hands are lightly placed behind the ears and the athlete then lifts the shoulders (not the lower back) and twists to one side, holding the position for three seconds before relaxing back down to the ground. The next repetition is to the other side, and so on.

Kneeling alternate-arm/leg raises – 2/2

See above.

Kneeling rotations – 6/6; 9/9; 12/12

This is an excellent exercise for improving the rotating core muscles as well as increasing this range of movement. The athlete kneels with

the hips forward and body upright. From here, one arm is taken round the back of the body with the hand hitting the ground between the feet. This arm is then flexed so that further rotation is created. While this is happening, the other arm wraps across the body in the direction of rotation. The final position is held for three seconds and then the body is rotated in the opposite direction.

Kneeling alternate-arm/leg raises – 2/2

See above.

Body-upright lunges – 6/6; 9/9; 12/12

See page 47.

In this version the exercise is performed on the toes.

Kneeling alternate-arm/leg raises – 2/2

See above.

Double-arm dumb-bell sprint action – 10/10; 15/15; 20/20

See page 111.

Kneeling alternate-arm/leg raises – 2/2

See above.

Hip raises – 8; 10; 12

See page 47.

Hold the top position for three seconds.

Kneeling alternate-arm/leg raises – 2/2

See above.

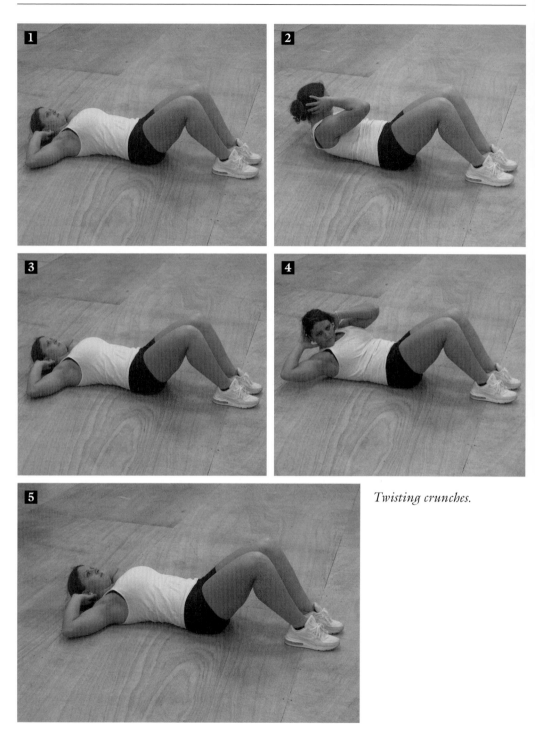

Twisting crunches.

Kneeling rotations.

Star jumps.

Session 2

Star jumps – 6; 8; 10

This is an old exercise but is effective as it uses virtually all the muscles in the body. At the start the athlete crouches with the hands touching the ground. From here, he or she drives upwards into a jump and then spreads the arms and legs into a 'star', bringing the limbs back together to land in the starting position.

Body-bridge alternate-leg lifts – 2/2

This is an advanced exercise with tremendous effects on the core stability muscles. The athlete sets up a body-bridge, with the arms vertical under the shoulders and the legs out straight. The body is held as near horizontal as possible and firm. Once this position has been attained, one leg is raised to the horizontal and held for eight seconds before lowering. The other leg is then raised similarly. This exercise is repeated after every other exercise in the session.

Press-ups – 5; 9; 12

See page 41.

Body-bridge alternate-leg lifts – 2/2

See above.

Alternate-leg 'V' sits – 5-5/8-8/12-12)

See page 31.

Body-bridge alternate-leg lifts – 2/2

See above.

Free twisting hyperextensions – 5/5; 8/8; 12/12

See page 31.

Body-bridge alternate-leg lifts – 2/2

See above.

Narrow-stance alternate-leg split jumps – 6/6; 8/8; 10/10

See page 26.

Body-bridge alternate-leg lifts – 2/2

See above.

Free sit-ups – 6; 9; 12

See page 31.

With no twist and the hands folded over the chest.

Body-bridge alternate-leg lifts – 2/2

See above.

Supported bounce jumps – 12; 20; 25

See page 38.

Body-bridge alternate-leg lifts – 2/2

See above.

Alternate-arm dumb-bell sprint arm action – 12/12; 20/20; 25/25

See page 111.

This should be over the whole range.

Body-bridge alternate-leg lifts.

Body-bridge alternate-leg lifts – 2/2

See above.

Squat thrusts – 8; 12; 15

See page 26.

Body-bridge alternate-leg lifts – 2/2

See above.

Full-arm body circling – 5/5; 8/8; 10/10

See page 26.

Body-bridge alternate-leg lifts – 2/2

See above.

Session 3

Burpees – 6; 9; 12

See page 38.

Kneeling alternate single-leg reverse raises – 2/2

This exercise is excellent for the lower back and core stability muscles of the mid-region. It is performed in a similar way to the kneeling alternate-arm/leg raise (*see* page 117) except that only the legs are lifted.

The athlete starts on all fours, the legs and arms placed vertically and the head held in a relaxed position, eyes down. From here, one leg at a time is raised behind and held for eight seconds. The legs are exercised alternately. This exercise should be repeated after every other exercise in the session.

Standing alternate-knee raises – 6/6; 9/9; 12/12

The effect of this exercise to is to improve hip-flexor strength and condition, as well as to improve balance. The athlete stands vertically with the arms raised directly in front of the shoulders. One leg is then raised so that the thigh is horizontal and the lower leg vertical. This position is held for three seconds, after which the athlete return to the start and raises the other leg similarly.

Kneeling alternate single-leg reverse raises – 2/2

See above.

Alternate-leg reverse raises – 6/6; 9/9; 12/12

See page 41.

Kneeling alternate single-leg reverse raises – 2/2

See above.

Free twisting sit-ups – 5/5; 8/8; 10/10

See page 31.

The arms should be held across the chest.

Kneeling alternate single-leg reverse raises – 2/2

See above.

Full-range leg raises – 8; 12; 15

This exercise is best performed on a slight incline to keep the stress on the rectus abdominis constant, although it is easier to do on the flat. The athlete lies on the ground and

127

Standing alternate-knee raises.

Full-range leg raises.

Narrow-grip press-ups.

may if necessary hold on to a bench or other non-movable object. With the legs slightly flexed to avoid excess strain on the lower back, the legs are smoothly raised and passed over the head to touch the hands. Some runners find this difficult because of stiffness in the back, but with perseverance the full range can be achieved.

Kneeling alternate single-leg reverse raises – 2/2

See above.

Narrow-grip press-ups – 6; 9; 12

This is a variation on the normal press-up. In this instance the elbows are tucked into the sides and the hands placed directly under the shoulders. This forces the triceps and deltoids to do most of the work when the body is lowered and then pushed up again.

Kneeling alternate single-leg reverse raises – 2/2

See above.

Narrow-stance alternate bounce jumps – 10/10; 15/15; 20/20

In bounce jumps the feet are normally placed shoulder-width apart. In this variation the feet are placed one in front of the other and are changed in mid-air during each repetition. This makes the front of the thighs do most of the work as opposed to the upper thigh in the wider stance. It is important that the athlete does not try to 'pike' forward on landing but instead bends the legs and keeps the body upright. An alternative, to keep the body upright, is to support the jump by holding a wall bar or beam in front during the movement (supported narrow-stance alternate bounce jumps).

Kneeling alternate single-leg reverse raises – 2/2

See above.

Feet-raised crunches – 6; 9; 12

This is another variation of crunches. In this exercise the athlete lies on his or her back with the legs slightly flexed, crossed and held off the ground. The shoulders are then raised and held for three seconds before relaxing back to the starting position.

Kneeling alternate single-leg reverse raises – 2/2

See above.

Knee-tuck jumps – 6; 9; 12

See page 41.

Kneeling alternate single-leg reverse raises – 2/2

See above.

Flat hyperextensions – 8; 12; 16

This is the most basic of the back hyperextension exercises, yet is simple and effective in working the lower back, gluteals and hamstrings. The athlete lies flat on the ground at the start, with the hands held lightly behind the ears. The shoulders and thighs are raised off the ground and held in that position for three seconds, then they are lowered and the exercise is repeated.

Kneeling alternate single-leg reverse raises – 2/2

See above.

131

Narrow-stance alternate bounce jumps.

Feet-raised crunches.

*Flat
hyperextensions.*

POST-TREATMENT REHABILITATION CONDITIONING

Post-treatment rehabilitation is the most important aspect of recovery from injury, but it is very often missed out by overenthusiastic coaches and athletes who want to return to the fray as soon as they can. The term means what it says: it is the process of reconditioning the injured area and the rest of the body after the injury has been treated. This kind of training lies very much in the realm of the specialist strength and conditioning expert.

The key to recuperating from injury successfully is patience: patience in not taking things too fast; patience in assessing what progress has been made; and patience in initially analyzing what needs to be done in terms of conditioning training to bring the athlete back into a fully functional state. There are three basic stages to recovery:

1. Treatment of the injury to a fully or near-painless state.
2. Post-treatment rehabilitation.
3. A progressive return to full training.

If any of these stages is omitted, there is a very high chance that the injury will reoccur or never fully heal. Too often athletes are repeatedly injured, usually in the same weak areas. Proper post-treatment rehabilitation is essential if this is to be avoided and is made up of three stages:

1. Analysing (with the help of the physiotherapist if necessary) exactly what muscle groups, joints or connective tissues are involved in the injury. Their state of repair and the intensity of conditioning the athlete can tolerate without causing a relapse can then be determined.
2. Designing circuits, part circuits or stage training sessions to suit the premise of reconditioning the athlete specifically as well as generally. The athlete's ability to perform the sessions should be tested carefully and the exercises modified if necessary.
3. Testing the injury by comparing it either with earlier results for the same limb (or area of the body) or with comparable results in an opposite limb. Only when the tests verify that the body part or area is up to full strength and conditioning level can usual training be resumed.

It is very important to control the intensity of any sessions, since most athletes who are either not performing well, or who have been injured, will be overenthusiastic. It is therefore a good idea to try the routine once through to see if any of the exercises cause pain or cannot physically be performed. If this is the case, further modifications are needed. The process of testing should then be repeated until a session is constructed that is hard and specific but can be performed by the athlete. From here, three steady circuits should be performed at each session, followed by a steady increase each week to six circuits; after this, timing can be introduced as a means of determining progress.

In some cases you might find that early on in recovery the injured area will need to be avoided altogether, in which instance the circuit can be modified to avoid those muscles or joints that are involved rather than work them. This will, of course, give only limited conditioning, but it will keep the athlete active and focused on recovering from his or her injury and getting back to full running.

In some rare cases an athlete cannot run at all but can perform gym work. In this instance a very effective procedure is to design a circuit that he or she is able to do that will have a general aerobic effect. That is, increase the number of exercises from eight or ten to fifteen, ensure they are performed for a longer period at a lower intensity, and use pulse rate

135

as an indicator. This is a very effective form of training since, like running, it involves the whole body. It is a far better way of maintaining and improving aerobic conditioning than the usual cycling and rowing as it can be made much more specific to running.

WHAT SHOULD BE TESTED?

The performance of the session itself will give the coach a strong indication as to what progress is being made. However, specific tests can be applied to the injured area in order to confirm the status of the athlete.

When an injury occurs, the blood flow to the region is disrupted. The first stage of healing involves the re-establishment of blood vessels so that nutrients can reach the site and waste products can be removed. However, these blood vessels will not be as numerous as they were before the injury, such that even the slightest exercise may bring on a painful reaction because oxygen simply cannot reach the muscles in the area. This is why it is vital not to push too hard at the beginning of the post-treatment period. Until the blood supply has been re-established, very little resistance should be applied during exercise.

The recovery of the circulation can easily be measured by recording how long the muscle can move for. In other words, taking the hamstrings as an example, you can compare how many repetitions the muscle group can perform with a minimal resistance compared with the other leg. Until the two are evenly matched it is reasonable to assume that full recovery has not taken place.

Once the circulation is back in place, the strengthening phase can be commenced. This involves increasing the resistance used during the movement, until again the injured and uninjured sides are comparable in ability. Finally, the specific movement coordination

needs to be restored by technical running. The speed of this can be increased gradually once the coach is satisfied that no imbalances remain. This training can be commenced during the strengthening phase and then moved up rapidly after full strength has been restored.

SAMPLE REHABILITATION SCHEME FOR A HAMSTRING INJURY

The hamstrings are commonly injured in running, be the cause a change of pace, cramp or a general postural imbalance. Most often they are damaged acutely, which is to say instantaneously rather than over a longer time frame. The torn fibres and the bleeding around the tear cause pain, swelling and a very marked reduction in the ability to straighten the leg without discomfort.

The treatment hopefully will proceed immediately, even before medical diagnosis, with the application of ice packs. On the assumption that a muscle tear is indicated, careful physiotherapy management is put into place until full range of movement is regained and the site is free of pain. The rehabilitation scheme should be implemented immediately, and should consist of the following:

1. A modified circuit to maintain aerobic conditioning during injury treatment and through the early part of the post-rehabilitation period.
2. A modified body-weight stage training programme to maintain anaerobic conditioning during injury treatment and through the early part of the post-rehabilitation period.
3. Post-treatment specific weight training to stimulate circulatory recovery around the injury site.
4. Post-treatment specific weight training to regain balanced strength in the muscle.

These stages should be performed within the framework outlined in the table (*below*).

It is only with this careful approach to rehabilitation that further injury will be minimized and

Rehabilitation activities

During treatment	Post-treatment to circulatory recovery	Post-treatment to strength regain	Build-up to full training	Full training
Modified circuit to maintain aerobic fitness	Modified circuit to maintain aerobic fitness	Modified circuit to maintain aerobic fitness, but with injured leg reintroduced into exercises	Full circuit session	Full circuit session
Modified body-weight stage training session to maintain anaerobic condition	Modified body-weight stage training session to maintain anaerobic condition	Modified body-weight stage training session to maintain anaerobic condition, but with injured leg reintroduced into exercises	Full body-weight stage training session	Full body-weight stage training session
	Specific weight training to assist in reinvesting the muscle with blood supply	Specific weight training to assist in reinvesting the muscle with blood supply		
		Specific weight training to strengthen the injured muscle to the equivalent of other leg		
			Full, balanced weight programme, building up to former levels (*see* Chapter 8)	Full, balanced or maintenance weights programme to continue, increase or maintain strength levels as necessary

the original problem solved in a satisfactory manner. If the process is rushed or parts are omitted, the chances of reinjury increase, which may in turn lead to the formation of scar tissue that will need to be removed by surgery. The treatment stages in the table on page 137 are discussed in more detail below.

MODIFIED CIRCUIT

A modified circuit to maintain aerobic condition is required during injury treatment and in the early part of the post-treatment rehabilitation period. In order to speed up a return to full training, it is vital that the athlete has worked around the injury and maintained the highest possible level of aerobic conditioning throughout the remaining functional parts of the body during the treatment period and into the start of the post-treatment rehabilitation phase.

Below is a sample circuit session that will help to keep the athlete fit but not overstress the injured hamstring. While careful flotation jacket work and other useful strategies can also be used, this type of session will have excellent stimulatory effects on the whole body without necessitating specialist apparatus. The session given here will help to maintain general aerobic fitness if performed in the usual way, keeping the heart rate at around 130–150 at the end of each exercise, with no recovery between exercises. Emphasis should be placed on keeping the body balanced, as the injury will tend to produce its own postural and action imbalances.

Press-ups

See page 41.

Feet-raised crunches

See page 131.

Single-leg reverse leg raises

These are similar to flat alternate-leg reverse raises (*see* page 41), except that only one leg is exercised.

Flat feet-held sit-ups

These are similar to free sit-ups (*see* page 31), except that the feet are held on the ground by a fellow athlete or hooked under a bar to make the exercise easier.

One-leg half-squats

These are performed by standing on one leg, with the injured leg held off the ground in front and the hands also raised in front. The good leg is then bent halfway and then extended. If balance is difficult, the arms can rest on a support but must not be used to aid movement.

Feet-raised bench dips

See page 31.

The injured leg is relaxed on the ground.

Alternate-arm dumb-bell sprint arm action

See page 111

Alternate the forward leg.

One-leg supported bounce jumps

See page 38.

Again, the injured leg is not used.

Many variations on this sample session can be developed to keep the circuit interesting and wide ranging.

MODIFIED BODY-WEIGHT STAGE TRAINING SESSION

To maintain anaerobic conditioning during injury treatment and in the early part of the post-treatment rehabilitation period, a modified programme of body-weight stage training can be developed. The emphasis of such a session can be towards any weak area of the body (apart from the injured area) that the coach determines might benefit the athlete's eventual progress. This is an ideal time to work on such weaknesses as it helps the athlete to focus on something other than being injured. The example given below assumes the hamstring-injured athlete also has less than satisfactory conditioning of the central abdominal muscles.

Narrow-stance dumb-bell split squats – 4 × 10/10

This simple exercise brings a more specific aspect to the squat movement, in that the whole legs are used in a similar way to running. The athlete stands with dumb-bells in hand, by the sides. The feet are split forward and backward, the back toes in line with the front heel. From here, the athlete squats down, keeping the back as vertical as possible and allowing the heels to lift to enable this. Once the low point is reached, the athlete then extends the legs vigorously back to the start position.

Feet-raised crunches – 1 × 10

See page 131.

This exercise is repeated after every other exercise in the session.

Feet-raised bench dips – 4 × 10

See page 31.

Feet-raised crunches – 1 × 10

See page 131

Chinnies – 4 × 8/8

See page 26.

Feet-raised crunches – 1 × 10

See page 131.

Kneeling alternate-leg/arm reverse raises – 4 × 12

See page 117.

Only the good leg should be used.

Feet-raised crunches – 1 × 10

See page 131.

Squats to toes – 4 × 10

Squats to toes extend the effect of a normal squat in that when the athlete drives from the low position, he or she follows the quadriceps extension with a powerful calf drive so that the finish point is on the toes. This trains the coordinated action between the thighs and calves, which is similar to the action performed during running. Note that the exercise must be done smoothly.

Feet-raised crunches – 1 × 10

See page 131.

Double-arm dumb-bell sprint arm action – 4 × 15/15

See page 111.

THIS PAGE:
Narrow-stance dumb-bell split squats.

OPPOSITE PAGE:
Squats to toes.

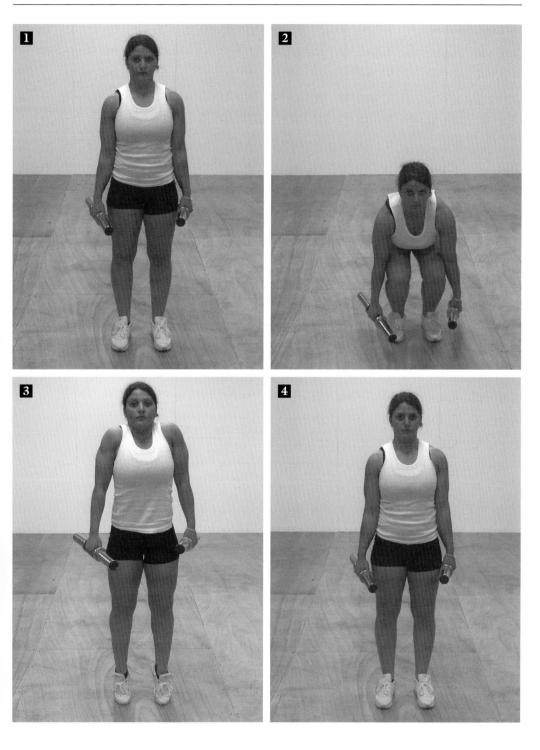

Feet-raised crunches – 1 × 10

See page 131.

Flat feet-held sit-ups – 4 × 10

See page 138.

Feet-raised crunches – 1 × 10

See page 131.

Full-arm body circling – 4 × 8/8

See page 26.

Feet-raised crunches – 1 × 10

See page 131.

This session is hard but will improve the front abdominal muscles as well as the other specific areas on which the individual exercises focus. The repetitions can be modified to suit the athlete, either by increasing or decreasing them as necessary. Once full rehabilitation has been achieved, the session can be modified to restore its original balanced theme in order to continue the specific abdominal improvement. The session is an example of how set results can be achieved, and can be used by coaches or athletes as a starting point for developing their own sessions depending on need.

SUMMARY

- The use of circuit training and body-weight stage training can be a godsend to the coach and runner during periods of specific problems or injury. They provide the means to continue both aerobic and local anaerobic training, and will not only keep enthusiasm going but can also actually improve other areas of weakness or bad conditioning.
- The sessions must be carefully planned to ensure that they do not make an injury worse. With analysis and design, however, the coach can be certain that the runner will at least be able to perform useful training by working around the problem even if it is another few weeks before track or road training can resume.
- The most important thing to remember is that training need not stop because a single body part is out of action, and that circuit and body-weight sessions can be used to fill the gap.

CHAPTER 8

General and Specific Weight Training

Weight training for marathon and endurance runners is nothing new. Most of the great runners have used weights during their training and it would seem that doing so also extends racing careers. Weight training is a universally accepted means of working the muscles hard and produces increases in muscle strength and size, as well as local endurance and general endurance ability.

But – and it's a big but – if weights are used incorrectly they can be very detrimental to the endurance athlete by causing an increase in muscle size in areas that are of little use. It is therefore essential for the runner to use tried and tested exercises that will be of most benefit during the running action. In addition, the way the exercises are performed has considerable bearing on their effectiveness.

GENERAL WEIGHT-TRAINING PRINCIPLES

Although training with heavy weights will enhance power, the athlete must ascertain the balance that is needed through the main part of the event in which he or she competes. For example, the 800m runner requires great power to perform the accelerations that are part of the top-level performer's arsenal of tactics. The marathon runner, however, never needs that fierce acceleration, but instead must be able to sprint and vary pace at a lower level. Therefore, the weight training for each, although similar in content, will be performed differently.

To understand why this is so, the nature of the effects of weight training must be explained. If we take the two extremes of such training – single-repetition maximum-resistance lifting (for example, ten sets of one repetition) versus high-repetition low-resistance training (for example, four sets of fifty repetitions) – these effects become very obvious. A single repetition with a maximum weight has no endurance effects and works the fast-twitch muscle fibres near maximally. This causes some muscle breakdown and therefore produces a mainly muscle-strengthening effect without any increase in endurance ability. In contrast, high-repetition low-resistance training has a completely different effect in that it utilizes the slow-twitch muscle fibres, thus improving the endurance part of the muscular system. Because the resistance is light, it does not break down muscle significantly and therefore has little effect on muscle bulk and strength.

The whole range of options between these two extremes produces mixed gradations of effect. As the resistance decreases and the repetitions increase, first strengthening (one to

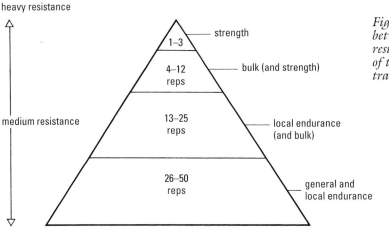

heavy resistance

strength — 1–3

4–12 reps — bulk (and strength)

medium resistance

13–25 reps — local endurance (and bulk)

26–50 reps — general and local endurance

light resistance

Fig. 9 The relationship between repetitions and resistance, and the effects of the two during weight training.

three repetitions) and then bulking (four to twelve repetitions) occur, after which come local muscular endurance specific to the muscles used (thirteen to twenty-five repetitions) and general aerobic changes (twenty-five or more repetitions). It is therefore vital that the correct method of weight training is chosen to produce the desired effect on the muscles and body.

Fig. 9 shows the effect repetitions and resistance have on the muscles. Obviously, this is just a simplification, but a knowledge of it does give the coach and athlete a way of working out the details of the weight schedule in order to produce the desired effect. Basically, the heavier the resistance, the lower the number of repetitions must be and the greater the strengthening effect produced. Conversely, the lighter the resistance, the higher the number of repetitions can be and therefore the greater the general aerobic effect produced.

Endurance runners should work primarily in the range of between fifteen and fifty repetitions, as this will have a local muscular endurance (anaerobic) effect at the lower end and a general aerobic effect at the upper end.

However, it is not only the way the exercises are done but also which exercises are performed that will determine their benefit or otherwise to the runner.

Two classes of weight-training exercises will benefit endurance runners. The first are general exercises and the second are more specific. General exercises can be used by the runner to improve the relevant larger muscle groups, while the more specific ones can help improve more select areas.

The exercises listed in this chapter are described in more detail in the companion title to this book, *Strength Training for Athletes*, also published by Crowood.

GENERAL WEIGHT-TRAINING EXERCISES FOR RUNNERS

Examples of general exercises are as follows:

1. Back squat.
2. Front squat.
3. Power clean.
4. Power snatch.

5. Press behind neck.
6. Bench dips (with resistance).
7. 'V' sits (with resistance).
8. Inclined twisting sit-ups (with resistance).
9. Flat twisting-back hyperextensions (with resistance).
10. Bench back hyperextensions (with resistance).
11. Leg bicep curls, double legs (full range).

All these exercises are used by athletes to elicit general strength as well as local muscular endurance improvement in the larger muscle groups of the body. For his or her part, the endurance athlete needs to perform them only during the preparation phases of the year and then only once a week thereafter for maintenance.

SPECIFIC WEIGHT-TRAINING EXERCISES

By using weight-training exercises specifically aimed at runners in the post-preparation periods, any general strength and local endurance gains will be maintained while the athlete is tuning into the more specific aspects of his or her events. Exercises that can achieve these goals are listed below, arranged according to the muscles or muscle groups they work.

Front of leg

1. Narrow-stance split squats and alternate split jumps.
2. Wide-stance split squats and alternate split jumps.
3. Narrow-stance front and back squats, squats to toes and squat jumps.
4. Supported bounce jumps (feet together or in alternate split positions).
5. Step-ups, step-up drives and step-in step-up drives.

Rear of leg

1. Leg bicep curls, alternate or single legs.
2. Straight single-leg front-to-back pull-throughs against resistance or Cliniband.
3. Lying reverse double-leg and alternate-leg raises.
4. Hip raises and leg extensions from the hip-raised position.

Body core – front and sides

1. Alternate-leg 'V' sits (with resistance).
2. Chinnies (with resistance).
3. Standing disc rotations.
4. Feet-raised twisting crunches and sit-ups (with resistance).
5. Dumb-bell side bends.
6. Hanging alternate-leg knee tucks (with resistance).
7. Knee-tuck jumps (with resistance).
8. Twisting sit-backs (with resistance).

Body core – lower back

1. Lying alternate reverse leg raises (with resistance).
2. Flat and bench twisting-back hyperextensions (with resistance).
3. Hanging hyperextensions (with resistance).
4. Leg bicep curls, single alternate legs.
5. Straight single-leg front-to-back pull-throughs against resistance or Cliniband.
6. Bent-over reverse dumb-bell raises.

Shoulders and arms

1. Standing and seated alternate dumb-bell press.
2. Single alternate-arm and double-arm sprint action.
3. Standing, forward, lateral and reverse arm dumb-bell raises.

4. Bent-arm flying exercise.
5. Dips and bench dips (with resistance).

All these exercises can be performed simply in a standard gymnasium with free weights. As always, safety comes first when weight training, and athletes must make sure they have good flat shoes, clothing that is not too loose and a weight-lifting belt. The focus should be on completing the sessions – as well and as quickly as possible. A simple short, effective schedule can be constructed by choosing one exercise from each section, thus covering all the relevant body segments. More exercises from a particular group can be chosen if one body area needs to be emphasized or rehabilitated, as seen in the example below.

SAMPLE SESSION FOR HAMSTRING WEAKNESS

A sample session for a runner with weak hamstrings might be as follows. The resistances suggested should increase steadily over time.

Narrow stance back squats – 20kg; 4 × 15

Leg bicep curls, alternate single legs – 2.5kg; 4 × 15/15

It is essential that this is performed over the full range.

Alternate-leg 'V' sits – 1kg; 4 × 10/10

Lying alternate-leg reverse raises – 1kg; 4 × 10/10

There should be a two-second hold at the top.

Hanging back hyperextensions – 1kg; 4 × 15

There should be a two-second hold at the top. Note also that lifting straps should be used to hold the athlete's grip to the overhead bar during this exercise as most will have difficulty with their grip.

Seated alternate dumb-bell press – 5kg; 4 × 15/15

For a local muscular endurance effect, the exercises should be performed with a light resistance in four sets of fifteen to twenty-five repetitions, and each set should be followed by alternate single-limb or twisting exercises. The aim is to increase the number of repetitions by one each week from the starting point.

For a more general aerobic effect, a very light resistance should be used in four sets of thirty repetitions, and again each set should be followed by the alternate single-limb or twisting exercises. The number of repetitions is increased by four per week up to a hundred. Resistance should not be increased unless, of course, it is obviously too light, the aim instead being to work on maintaining excellent technique throughout the sets.

SUMMARY

- Weight training for endurance athletes can significantly improve performance, particularly in relation to posture and the ability to move faster when needed. General exercises can help build the platform from which the champion will spring.
- More specific weight-training work can help to correct imbalances and aid rehabilitation from injury, and is the best way to achieve fast and effective results in these areas.

CHAPTER 9

Assessing Progress

Assessing an athlete's progress in terms of conditioning requires a detailed knowledge of where he or she was, is and wants to be. The problem with this is that everyone is an individual with distinct strengths and weaknesses, imbalances and problems, so comparisons are valid only in broad general terms and between similar measurements and assessments of the same individual.

The real measure of progress is whether the athlete competes better as a result of the conditioning and specific training he or she does, as this tests all the elements of the work in a combined sense. The coach and runner must, however, be able to measure whether or not the effect of a particular type of conditioning is actually what was intended, although care must be taken to ensure that the tests do not become the end rather than the means.

Rather than discussing the details of intricate physiological laboratory testing, this chapter looks at practical on-track methods that are available to, and easily used by, anyone. At the higher levels of competition in particular, it is important for some laboratory testing to be done, although this can be supplemented with on-track assessment.

GENERAL AEROBIC ABILITY TESTS

Aerobic fitness is needed to perform an activity over an extended period of time. The sim-plest test of aerobic ability therefore measures how fast an athlete can run for such a period. This can be done simply by keeping records of the runner's personal best times for various distances both on the track and on the road. The level being achieved and the degree of progress can then be ascertained.

As described in Chapter 2, the measurement of VO_2max (maximum oxygen uptake) is essential for athletes at the top level. An accurate assessment will enable the runner to work out how training is going by seeing what percentage of the VO_2max can be sustained and for how long. This is of great significance in longer events, as the higher the percentage of VO_2max at which the athlete runs, the greater the consumption of body energy resources (in particular carbohydrates) and the higher the level of lactic acid production. The careful control of this particular aspect of the run can therefore have very beneficial effects on the eventual result, whereas ignoring it may prove disastrous.

AT THE TRACK OR GYMNASIUM

A number of tests that can be carried out in the gym or on the track are available for VO_2max. These are inherently less accurate than those based in the laboratory but can be used to measure initial levels and subsequent improvements. Two of the most often used are described here.

The Beep Test

The multi-stage fitness test, also known as the bleep test or shuttle-run test, is used by sports coaches and trainers to estimate an athlete's VO_2max. The test is especially useful for players of sports like football, hockey or rugby. As it is designed to measure the maximum endurance of an individual, the test should not be carried out on anyone with low fitness levels.

The test involves running continuously between two points that are set 20m apart. These runs are synchronized with a pre-recorded audio tape or CD, which plays beeps at set intervals. As the test proceeds, the interval between each successive beep reduces, forcing the athlete to increase velocity over the course of the test, until it is impossible to keep in sync with the recording.

The recording is typically structured into twenty-three levels, each of which lasts sixty seconds. Usually, the interval of beeps is calculated to require a speed of 8.5km/h at the start, increasing by 0.5km/h with each level. The progression from one level to the next is signalled by three rapid beeps. The highest level the athlete attains before he or she is unable to keep up is recorded as the score for that test.

The Cooper Test

The Cooper test is a test of physical fitness and was designed by Kenneth H. Cooper in 1968 for US military use. In its original form, the point of the test is to run as far as possible within twelve minutes. It is meant to measure the condition of the participant and is therefore supposed to be run at a steady pace rather than a series of sprints.

The results of the test give a rough estimate of condition, with possible outcomes being 'very good', 'good', 'average', 'bad' and 'very bad'. These outcomes are reached according to distance run, age and gender (*see* table opposite), and the results also correlate well with VO_2max measurements (*see* below). In general, the Cooper test is very easy and cheap to run, especially for larger groups. Its drawbacks are that the results are based on the motivation of the person taking it and practice is required.

As mentioned above, Cooper test results correlate quite well with VO_2max data, using the formula below:

$$VO_2max = (\text{distance in metres} - 505) \div 45$$

IN THE LABORATORY

For serious runners, laboratory testing for VO_2max is an essential. Not only will such tests give accurate results, but they can also be used to follow changes in the body over a long period of training, giving ready indicators of success or failure.

VO_2max Test

The laboratory VO_2max test involves performing a graded exercise on a stationary exercise machine. The test starts at a very easy level and increases in intensity in one-minute stages until the participant can no longer continue. The subject's nose is plugged, so that he or she breathes entirely through a mouthpiece connected to a metabolic analyser, and he or she also wears a heart-rate monitor. The analyser measures the volume of air breathed as well as the percentage of carbon dioxide and oxygen in the expired gas.

The VO_2max of the test participant is the volume of oxygen his or her body uses during one minute of maximal exercise. Expressed as litres of oxygen per minute or millilitres of oxygen per kilogram of bodyweight per minute, this data indicates and individual's potential for endurance athletics. While anaerobic threshold

Cooper test assessment tables

Ages 13–20

		Very good	Good	Average	Bad	Very bad
13–14	M	>2,700m	2,400–2,700m	2,200–2,399m	2,100–2,199m	<2,100m
	F	>2,000m	1,900–2,000m	1,600–1,899m	1,500–1,599m	<1,500m
15–16	M	>2,800m	2,500–2,800m	2,300–2,499m	2,200–2,299m	<2,200m
	F	>2,100m	2,000–2,100m	1,900–1,999m	1,600–1,699m	<1,600m
17–20	M	>3,000m	2,700–3,000m	2,500–2,699m	2,300–2,499m	<2,300m
	F	>2,300m	2,100–2,300m	1,800–2,099m	1,700–1,799m	<1,700m

Ages 20–50+

		Very good	Good	Average	Bad	Very bad
20–29	M	>2,800m	2,400–2,800m	2,200–2,399m	1,600–2,199m	<1,600m
	F	>2,700m	2,200–2,700m	1,800–2,199m	1,500–1,799m	<1,500m
30–39	M	>2,700m	2,300–2,700m	1,900–2,299m	1,500–1,899m	<1,500m
	F	>2,500m	2,000–2,500m	1,700–1,999m	1,400–1,699m	<1,400m
40–49	M	>2,500m	2,100–2,500m	1,700–2,099m	1,400–1,699m	<1,400m
	F	>2,300m	1,900–2,300m	1,500–1,899m	1,200–1,499m	<1,200m
50+	M	>2,400m	2,000–2,400m	1,600–1,999m	1,300–1,599m	<1,300m
	F	>2,200m	1,700–2,200m	1,400–1,699m	1,100–1,399m	<1,100m

Experienced Competitive Athletes

	Very good	Good	Average	Bad	Very bad
M	>3,700m	3,400–3,700m	3,100–3,399m	2,800–3,099m	<2,800m
F	>3,000m	2,700–3,000m	2,400–2,999m	2,100–2,399m	<2,100m

is the best predictor of current endurance performance, VO_2max shows what the athlete could achieve after several years of systematic, structured training. For those who take the test to completion, the resulting data can be used to calculate the true VO_2max.

Onset of Blood Lactate Test

This test determines the onset of blood lactate (OBL) during exercise, which can help to determine an appropriate training intensity and monitor progress in the serious athlete. This test is similar to the VO_2max test, but with slightly longer periods of time between changes in workload – it is not always considered a maximal test but does require a high intensity of effort. The test involves taking several blood samples from the finger or ear for the assessment of blood lactate.

From the measurements of blood lactate taken during the test, a graph is constructed to show how levels change as the intensity of running increases (*see* Fig. 10). The graph exhibits three important thresholds:

1. The aerobic threshold, which is the intensity of running at which the blood lactate starts to increase linearly from resting levels (around 1mmol/ltr in Fig. 10), and the intensity or heart rate at which an individual burns most fat. Using fat for fuel, more oxygen is required to release a given amount

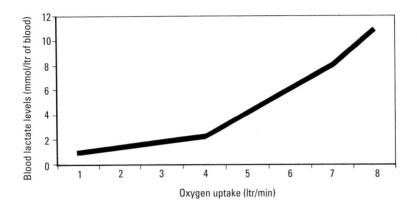

Fig. 10 Determining lactate threshold.

of energy than when carbohydrate is the main fuel. This means that at low intensities, when plenty of oxygen is available to the muscle, fat is the preferred fuel. As intensity increases, at some point the cardiovascular system will not be able to transport proportionally more oxygen to the muscles. This is the aerobic threshold; above this point, increased exercise intensity will lead to a reduction in fat burning.

2. The anaerobic threshold, which is the point on the graph when the blood lactate starts to increase non-linearly (around 4mmols/ltr). Endurance athletes know this as the 'red line', and it is the highest intensity, as measured by heart rate, at which the body can remove lactic acid as quickly as it is produced. Just below the anaerobic threshold, an athlete is working hard but feels no burning in the muscles, and is breathing heavily but in a controlled way. Above the anaerobic threshold, however, lactic acid builds up in the muscles and causes premature fatigue. Knowing one's threshold allows a very high level of cardiovascular conditioning to be achieved without the discomfort and muscle damage that result from a lactic acid build-up.

3. The VO_2max, which is the maximum level of oxygen uptake that can attained (the end of the graph).

The Bruce protocol			
Stage	Duration (minutes)	Speed (km/h)	Incline (%)
1	3	2.7	10
2	3	4.0	12
3	3	5.5	14
4	3	6.7	16
5	3	8.0	18
6	3	8.8	20
7	3	9.6	22

OBL testing takes place on a treadmill and is set up according to either the normal or modified Bruce protocol. The normal Bruce protocol was invented to test the general public for heart problems and consists of a series of seven three-minute runs on the treadmill. During each period, the speed and incline are increased (*see* table (*above*) for the details).

Because so many tests using this protocol have been performed, it is now possible to use the results to predict VO_2max to a reasonable degree of accuracy. This calculation is not as accurate as a proper laboratory VO_2max test, but it can be a useful and straightforward way to check a runner's progress. The formula used is as follows:

The modified Bruce protocol.		
Stage	Duration (minutes)	Speed (km/h)
1	3	6.4
2	3	9.6
3	3	11.2
4	3	12.9
5	3	14.5
6	3	16.1
7	3	17.7
8	3	19.3
9	3	20.9
10	3	22.5
11	3	24.1
12	3	25.7

$$VO_2max = 14.76 - (1.38 \times [\text{max. running time}]) + (0.451 \times [\text{max. running time}]^2) - (0.12 \times [\text{max. running time}]^3)$$

The modified Bruce protocol was subsequently developed specifically for endurance runners, and can be seen in the table (*above*). At every interval, the oxygen uptake and blood lactate levels are measured and then plotted on a graph to ascertain the aerobic and anaerobic threshold levels. Although the results are of some importance initially, they are particularly useful when repeat measurements are taken during the training year, as they give an excellent indication of how effective the training has been. If the whole graph shifts to the right, the athlete is definitely making progress.

RANGE OF MOVEMENT TESTS

The importance of range of movement (ROM) has been discussed in Chapter 5. A runner can perform optimally only if he or she has adequate ROM in the joints to allow a relaxed and comfortable posture while running.

Obviously, range of movement is reasonably specific to an event, but nevertheless a good basic range in all joints will have the best effect when trying to minimize energy consumption. For the runner, the key areas are the ankles, knees, hips, back and shoulders. All these regions of the body come under stress during running events, and the ability to achieve good ROM will enhance the achievement of good technique. Ranges of movement for these areas of the body can be assessed in the gym, as described below.

Ankles

The ROM of the ankles can effectively be measured by determining the angle between the shin bone and the foot in either direction. Normally, athletes have no problem with pointing the foot, but flexing the ankle is sometimes difficult because of a shortening of the Achilles tendon. To measure ankle flexion, the foot is placed firmly and flat on the ground and the knee is pushed forward. The angle between the shin and foot can then simply be measured with a large protractor. As an indication, a 90-degree angle between the shin and foot is very poor, 80–70 degrees is average and <60 degrees is good. If the measurement is towards the poorer end of the range, urgent attention must given to improving it as running technique will be adversely affected by the limitation.

Knees

There is rarely a problem with ROM in the knees except at the extreme ends of the range. Long-distance runners tend not to extend the knee fully during their event, or to use full flexion. This lack of movement at the ends of the range becomes ingrained after a period, to the point where it is a clinical problem. It is therefore vital for such athletes to work the full range in their preparatory conditioning when not out running. Again, the ROM angles can be measured with a large protractor, when the athlete is standing and squatting down fully.

Hips

A lack of ROM in the hips is a major cause of poor results in running events. Such a problem is usually caused by tight hamstrings or hip flexors and must be rectified urgently.

Measuring the ROM in the hips is difficult because they tend to rotate when the surrounding muscles are tight, thus giving a false impression of the true state of play. It is therefore essential when making such an assessment to ensure that the hips remain fixed while the legs move around them. This is best achieved in the lying position when the connected muscles are relaxed. The angles of flexion (knee to chest) and extension (knee moving to the rear) should both be measured. A good range for the former is around 135 degrees from the flat, while anything around 90 degrees shows that there is severe limitation of movement, something that needs to be addressed immediately. In the extension range, 0–10 degrees from the flat is a poor measurement and again needs attention, whereas 30–40 degrees is very good.

Lateral hip ROM is also important, although in the vast majority of cases it is not a problem. A normal athlete should be able to do a sideways split to beyond 90 degrees, but if he or she cannot achieve this then some work needs to be done to remedy the situation

Back

Problems with the back tend to be related to posture rather than range of movement. Many runners have very bad back posture, which can be seen simply by observing him or her from the side and back while he or she is standing and running. If there are any unnatural curves, either laterally or vertically, then remedial conditioning should be added to the schedule. If problems persist, it is advisable to consult a physiotherapist to ensure that there are no underlying physical abnormalities. Poor back positions tend to cause major problems lower down the body, particularly in the hamstrings, so it is well worth paying attention to this area.

Shoulders

Many runners pay little attention to this area of their body and as a consequence allow stiffness and a reduced range of movement to become the norm. This often results in poor running technique, with a consequent inability to run in a relaxed and good postural way.

The ROM angles of the shoulders are easily measured in the standing or lying position. Taking the arms forward and up over the head should be accomplished in a comfortable fashion to a point where they are in line with the body. Any ROM that is noticeably less than this needs to be corrected, as it will create tension in the shoulders while running. Taking the arms back and up should bring them to an angle of 80–90 degrees to the body. Again, any range less than this must be improved to ensure a relaxed running action.

LOCAL MUSCULAR ENDURANCE TESTS

Injury causes a reduction in the capillarization (blood supply) of the affected area, which in turn reduces the local endurance of the associated muscles or muscle groups. As discussed in Chapter 7, it is vital that this local endurance is restored as soon as possible.

If conducted in the right way, simple weight exercises are an excellent test for progress in improvements to local muscular endurance. Taking a quadriceps tear as an example of an injury, progress can be assessed using the seated leg-extension movement. In this the athlete sits upright on a bench and isolates the quadriceps by not allowing any forward or backward movement of the body. The good leg is tested first and a light weight (probably in the region of 5–10kg) is used for the resistance. The athlete then completes as many repetitions as possible. The time taken for these to be completed is recorded, after which the athlete rests for the same amount of time before trying the exercise on the injured leg.

During the early stages of recovery from injury, there will be a marked difference between the two legs. This will gradually disappear over a period of about three weeks, during which time the blood supply is being restored. When the two legs can achieve the same amount of work in the same time, the repair is complete and normal training can resume. This method of testing can be applied to any muscle or muscle group with the use of appropriate exercises.

REACTIVE ABILITY TESTS

Although reactive ability is not a major essential for the long-distance runner, the ability to sprint at the end of a race may be very significant for middle-distance runners and even long-distance runners in a sprint-finish scenario. A runner cannot sprint effectively unless this aspect of his or her ability is at least reasonable, which is why some form of test is useful to determine the state of play.

The simplest tests of reactive ability are standing jumps. Of these, the standing long jump and triple jump are the most effective for the runner. In the standing long jump, the athlete starts with the feet on the edge of a long-jump pit, then bends the legs and jumps into the pit for distance. A good level of performance would be around 2.6m for male runners and 2.3m for female runners. Anything below 2.2m and 2.0m respectively indicates very low reactive ability and the need for some plyometric conditioning. In the standing triple jump, distances of 7m for male runners and 6m for female runners would be expected. Jumps of less than 6m and 5m respectively point out the need for improvement.

SUMMARY

- To assess the status of an athlete and to ensure that his or her training is effective, it is essential that the various aspects of physical performance are tested as part of the schedule. The coach must set in place a sensible and meaningful programme of tests, and must then be able to understand the results and use them to modify and improve training.

- Athletes do not need to be tested every day or even every week, but the positive and careful use of a range of tests will not only pick up problems before they arise, but can also give the coach and athlete confidence that what they are doing is effective.

- Testing can be fun and is a useful tool for the coach. There are many more tests than those described above, but it is essential that 'fad' testing is not applied since this can often be meaningless and counterproductive. Tried and tested protocols should always be used so that the results obtained will be comparable and meaningful from month to month and from athlete to athlete.

CHAPTER 10

Workouts for Beginners and Fun-runners

Having been asked on many occasions what a newcomer to endurance running should do to avoid injury and improve performance, my answer is always the same: find out as much as you can about the basics of endurance training and ask as many people as you can what they have found works best for them. There are many ways to find the right path for you as an individual in the long term, but in general there are only a few basics that you need to learn and adhere to in order to have some success in the initial stages and to remain injury-free. Once you have had a medical check to make sure there are no underlying problems that might risk your health, the key requirements are as follows:

1. A basic aerobic fitness ability.
2. Good posture and technique while running.
3. Sound joints, mobility and suppleness.
4. A determination and mental strength to put up with the pain and occasional boredom that is inevitable when running long distances.
5. A basic knowledge of sports nutrition as applied to endurance events.
6. A good-quality pair of trainers that, if necessary, provide arch support (*see* Chapter 2).

BASIC AEROBIC FITNESS ABILITY

Everyone is different. This may seem self-evident, but when they start on the road to endurance running success many people honestly believe that they could be as good as Paula Radcliffe or Felix Limo. The differences between us are, however, very great, and we range from those who can hardly run a step even after much training to those who find it easy and can reach the very top in such events.

Most fun-runners and late-start marathon runners fall somewhere in the middle of the scale, having quite good aerobic ability but not to the extent that they are marked out as champions earlier in life. Although the urge to perform well is as strong in such runners as in the champions, their ability will not reflect this desire. Having said that, the correct preparation and training will allow such an individual to achieve his or her best results and so is well worth doing.

The best way to see if you are suited to running is to try it for three or four weeks. You should be able to decide within that time limit whether you can handle it or not, but make sure that you do not push yourself beyond the limit

Fun-runners.
(COURTESY OF WEBSHOTS.COM)

just to prove to yourself how good you are. And a word of warning: if you are quite overweight or extremely unfit, make sure you lose as much weight as possible before trying to run hard, and increase your basic aerobic level by starting off with plenty of walking rather than running.

Walking is much gentler on the joints but can be as aerobically testing as running if done at speed. It is a very good way of increasing aerobic work at a time when the joints are simply not up to taking the pounding that running would give them. Walking also strengthens the hamstrings, which are often weak and unconditioned in people who have done little running. Stiffness will result after walking, for a period of about two weeks from the day you start; once this goes, a gentle start can then be made on running.

THE FIRST STEPS

The table on page 156 gives an indication of how you can start on the road to endurance running. There will, of course, be great vari-

ation between people, so exercise care in what you attempt and how fast you progress. The eight-week programme is an average basic schedule, with three sessions per week. Increases and decreases in the walking and running times can be put in place, but do not exceed what you are reasonably capable of.

In addition to the first-steps running programme, a suppling session of fifteen minutes should be performed every other day as well as the loosening that is needed before any of the walking/running sessions are attempted. At the end of this period of basic training, you will know whether you want to continue or leave it there.

RUNNING POSTURE AND TECHNIQUE

As your ability to run improves, it will become increasingly important to ensure that your posture is good and that your running technique is efficient and will not lead to injury. One of the most important aspects of correct running

Basic first-step endurance running programme.

Session 1

Week 1	Week 2	Week 3	Week 4	Week 5	Week 6	Week 7	Week 8
Combination 2-min. walk/ 2-min. run for 16 mins	Combination 2-min. walk/ 3-min. run for 20 mins	Combination 2-min. walk/ 4-min. run for 24 mins	Combination 1-min. walk/ 5-minute run for 24 mins	Run for 7 mins, walk for 1 min., run for 7 mins – repeat	Run for 10 mins, walk for 1 min run for – repeat three times	Run for 12 mins, walk for 1 min – repeat three times	Run for 15 mins, walk for 1 min Run for 15 mins

Session 2

Week 1	Week 2	Week 3	Week 4	Week 5	Week 6	Week 7	Week 8
Combination 2-min. walk/ 2-min. run for 16 mins	Combination 2-min. walk/ 3-min. run for 20 mins	Combination 1-min. walk/ 4-min. run for 20 mins	Combination 1-min. walk/ 6-min. run for 28 mins	Run for 10 mins, walk for 1 min., run for 10 mins	Run for 12 mins, walk for 1 min., run for 12 mins	Run for 14 mins, walk for 2 min run for 14 mins	Run for 25 mins non-stop

Session 3

Week 1	Week 2	Week 3	Week 4	Week 5	Week 6	Week 7	Week 8
Combination 2-min. walk/ 2-min. run for 16 mins	Combination 2-min. walk/ 3-min. run for 20 mins	Combination 2-min. walk/ 4-min. run for 24 mins	Combination 1-min. walk/ 5-min. run for 25 mins	Run for 7 mins, walk for 1 min., run for 7 mins – repeat	Run for 10 mins, walk for 1 min., – repeat three times	Run for 12 mins, walk for 1 min., – repeat three times	Run for 15 mins, walk for 1 min., Run for 15 mins

technique is the position of the Achilles tendon in relation to the heel bone. Simple observation will tell you if you have a problem and whether you need arch support or other corrective orthotics to realign this tendon–bone axis. The best way to do this is to ask someone to look from the rear at your ankles and to mark on a piece of paper the angle at which the Achilles tendon attaches to the heel. If it is straight, there is not a problem, but if it angles out, arch support is almost definitely needed. If the tendon angles the other way, you should see a physiotherapist as an underlying physical problem may be the cause other than simple flat feet.

It is vital that the Achilles tendons are in alignment with the heel bones. If they are not, there will be a constant sheering force on the tendon that will inevitably lead to inflammation and possible permanent injury. Correctly assessed and fitted orthotics can resolve the problem rapidly, but if it persists you must have a repeat consultation as again there may be an underlying problem that needs urgent resolution before running resumes.

With regards to running action, this is best left to the expert eye of a running coach. This is why it is recommended that even at this early stage you join an athletics or running club so that you will receive the very best advice on how to go about achieving your desired result. The basics of good endurance running are to have a technique that is both efficient and posturally safe. You will often see athletes who look decidedly off-balance or awkward when they run, but if you specifically observe their actual running action, more often than not it will be smooth and strong. Runners often struggle with their upper body posture while being spot-on below the waist. This might sound contrary to what you would expect, but in essence the runner must find the best way to make his or her upper body help the legs do their job.

If you unsure of your own technique and do not have a coach, find someone to take video of you and watch the replay, comparing it with a video recording of a top-class runner. You will soon be able to spot the basic problems and differences, and even correcting these will help with your performance.

SOUND JOINTS, MOBILITY AND SUPPLENESS

One of the major problems for individuals starting their running career later in life is that their bones, joints, tendons and ligaments have not enjoyed a long period of adaptation to such exercise. Most of us did physical education at school and then left it well alone until the decision was made to run a 10km or marathon race. During the interim, those parts that enable our muscles to apply force may have weakened or even deteriorated to a dangerous level. It cannot be stressed too strongly that running is very hard on the joints of the back, hips and legs, and if any structural weakness is inherent in the runner, this activity will seek out and punish it.

Many runners push past the point of common sense and end up with serious structural injuries. It is, therefore, vital that before you even start to run you check out all the relevant joints of your body for full range of movement and then work on suppling the muscles, tendons and ligaments to a good level. If there is even a hint of a joint problem, have it looked at by a specialist before you embark on a sport that could potentially end up in damaging your body in the long term. During the period of pre-running when you are gearing your body up by walking aerobically, it is strongly recommended that you perform basic suppling every other day. This will ensure that by the time you commence your first step of running, you are aware that your body is ready, able and willing.

MENTAL STRENGTH AND CONDITIONING

In order to divert your mind from the pain and boredom associated with long-distance running, you need to have the correct mind-set in the first place. With the application of sophisticated psychological techniques a person can be changed, but if this is necessary you should ask yourself why you are putting yourself through such purgatory if it is not for you. This is not to say that you should not persevere when the going gets tough, but rather that those few of us who simply can't hack it would be better off choosing a different sport.

Toughness in running often comes through long practice, but some runners never achieve it even when they reach the highest level. The true greats are those who grit their teeth and fight on, whatever the circumstances, and it is fair to say that these people are born rather than created by training. Such performances as Sebastian Coe's comeback for gold in the 1,500m final at the 1980 Moscow Olympics, having lost the 800m to Steve Ovett, was hardly mortal. Not all of us are capable of such things, however, and even the plodding fun-runner needs some part of it in order to stay the course and achieve a degree of satisfaction from endurance running.

KNOWLEDGE OF SPORTS NUTRITION

A sound knowledge of basic sports nutrition can save a lot of heartache if applied correctly for long races. The body needs energy to perform the running action, and unless the supply is sufficient for the job, then clearly the race will not be completed easily.

Many theories about nutrition for endurance running have been put forwards, but most of these are untested and end up being wrong to the point that they detract from an athlete's performance. The basics of sports nutrition are simple:

1. Eat sufficient food but not too much, and ensure that your diet is balanced.
2. Drink enough but not too much, sticking to water as much as possible except during races, when specialist drinks can supply your extra carbohydrate needs at the right time.
3. Take modest vitamin and mineral supplements, but avoid highly concentrated foods such as protein and carbohydrate drinks unless you are in need of them, which will be seldom. Take supplements of the more exotic kind, such as glucosamine and chondroitin, only if they work as proven scientifically and are not illegal according to the rules of your sport.

An awful lot of rubbish on diet has been written for runners in the hope that it will be a magic recipe for success. Fortunately, most athletes have plenty of common sense and will not be taken in by false claims. A final piece of advice is to keep your diet simple and basic, and if you are in any doubt about something, don't take it, eat it or drink it.

MOVING FORWARD

Although most beginners and fun-runners will not want to spend time on conditioning for their sport, it is a key requirement for improvement. If you include some gym work in your schedule, you will reap the benefits in terms of improvement and a reduction in injuries. The information in previous chapters of this book will help to point you in the right direction.

SUMMARY

- If you are a newcomer to endurance running, take the utmost care in preparing yourself mentally and physically for what is to follow.
- Do not push yourself beyond the limit and do not tolerate pain in the hope that it will go away.
- Running can range from a wonderful experience to purgatory, through all grades in between. Be sensible in your approach, look after your body and enjoy what you do. Always err on the side of caution and base your efforts on sound knowledge or advice from a good coach.
- Remember that safety is more important to the beginner or fun-runner than performance levels.

Index